# GOD IN CONCORD

RICHARD GELDARD taught philosophy at Yeshiva University and is the author of *The Esoteric Emerson* and *The Vision of Emerson*. He holds a doctorate in Drama and Classics from Stanford University. He and his wife, the artist and writer Astrid Fitzgerald, divide their time between Manhattan and the Hudson Valley.

*Emerson in clerical garb, in his early thirties*

# GOD IN CONCORD

## Ralph Waldo Emerson's Awakening to the Infinite

RICHARD G. GELDARD

PUBLISHED FOR THE PAUL BRUNTON
PHILOSOPHIC FOUNDATION BY

LARSON PUBLICATIONS

International Standard Book Number: 0-943914-89-2
Library of Congress Catalog Card Number: 98-67552

Published for the Paul Brunton Philosophic Foundation by
Larson Publications
4936 NYS Route 414
Burdett, New York 14818 USA

05   04   03   02   01   00   99   98
10   9   8   7   6   5   4   3   2   1

FOR SALLY AND JENNIFER

DAUGHTERS OF CONCORD

∽

# CONTENTS

# ACKNOWLEDGMENTS

*This book* began to take shape as a direct result of philosophy classes at Yeshiva College in "The Science of Mind." Several persistent students pushed hard at the notion of the nature of consciousness and, together, we began to formulate ideas of mind, some of which emerged from Emerson's central essays on the topic. The question then arose, "What was the sequence and the progress in Emerson's own thinking about mind as he developed a vision of God, or the Infinite? In addition, several key ideas came from my earlier work, *The Esoteric Emerson*, published in 1993 by Lindisfarne Press.

I am indebted in the preparation of the manuscript to the staff of the Houghton Library and the Divinity School at Harvard University for access to their archives. As well, any scholar who seeks an understanding of Emerson's thought is deeply indebted to the dedicated editors of the sixteen-volume *Journals and Miscellaneous Notebooks* published by The Belknap Press. Without their attention to minute detail over nearly thirty years of work, any attempt to trace the development of Emerson's thought would be doomed to approximations.

Finally, I thank my wife, Astrid Fitzgerald, for guiding me through the subtleties of Eastern thought, and my editor, Paul Cash, for unparalleled attention to the manuscript. Any errors or lapses of clarity in the text are my own and would have been more egregious without his care and friendship.

*Emerson in his fifties*

# INTRODUCTION

*On May 25, 1903,* the small town of Concord, Massachusetts, hosted the Centenary Celebration of the birth of its most illustrious son, Ralph Waldo Emerson. The main speaker for the occasion was Professor William James of Harvard, who even today is thought of as the father of American philosophy. In a letter to a friend following his appearance, James said, "I let RWE. speak for himself. . . . Reading the whole of him over again continuously has made me feel his greatness as I never did before." In his remarks on that May afternoon, James set the tone for the appraisal of Emerson for the next fifty years.

> For Emerson, the individual fact and moment were indeed suffused with absolute radiance, but it was upon a condition that saved the situation—they must be worthy specimens,—sincere, authentic, archetypal; they must have made connection with what he calls the Moral Sentiment, they must in some way act as symbolic mouthpieces of the Universe's meaning. To know just which thing does act in this way, and which thing fails to make the true connection, is the secret (somewhat incommunicable, it must be confessed) of seership, and doubtless we must not expect of a seer too rigorous a consistency. Emerson himself was a real seer.[1]

We have today in Emerson's complete work—formal essays, private journals, notebooks, letters, sermons, early lectures, and the testimony of the contemporaries who shared his life—as accurate a gauge of the powers of a great mind as we could hope to possess. The sheer volume of these reflections, combined with his determination to penetrate to the core of things, opens a rare door into the life of one individual's profound seeking.

Emerson's work seems to grow as we do. First exposures to it, arising as they tend to do early in the development of the growing intellect, are generally superficial, the experiences of forced readings or youthful exuberance. The early reading experience is almost giddy and certainly fanciful. It seems to contradict daily experience; as a result we may conclude that whatever he is saying, daily experience is not part of the formula. We wonder what world he is describing. It certainly isn't the second half of the twentieth century. Second and third readings, however, stimulated from the existential perspective of our century's anxiety and failures of vision, offer a more solid basis of serious study. The work requires penetration, and more to the point, stands up to it.

As James said, Emerson was a seer. To be able to say now that Emerson's thought and seeing constitute revelation takes a certain amount of theological sleight-of-hand, but this book hopes to demonstrate one individual's high degree of gnostic understanding of the Abyss as an antidote to Post-modern cynicism. Emerson said flatly that "the best we can know of God is the mind as it is known to us." Knowing as much as we can of Emerson's mind allows us to project out into the chasm of the cosmos as far as minds can reach. That these simultaneously inward and outward glances take us well beyond the range of traditional religious thinking will be obvious enough once we follow the trail far enough.

Emerson began his task with a courageous, idealistic beginning in the 1830s. His articulated vision of a fully realized human being has not been completed. The vision was transmitted in a fragmented literary mode to a pitifully small audience prior to the Civil War. What we now call Emersonian Idealism grew into an intellectual movement only after 1903, the centennial of his birth, when the Complete Works were finally published and became widely known outside of New England.

After the Birth Centenary, the next major impulse in Emerson studies came in 1982, the centennial of his death. The literary output of the participants in this anniversary was biographical and not philosophical. Emerson the Writer and Emerson the Man were subjected to endless

Freudian analyzes and exercises in deconstruction. For the most part, he survived very nicely. Those books aimed at the general reader celebrated his life in all its earthy and emotional detail and revealed the struggle of a individual being true to his vision through life's trials and tragedies.

As we now approach 2003, the bicentennial of his birth on May 25, the next impulse may be to restore something of the philosophical validity to the wisdom literature. Steps in that important direction have already been taken by Harvard's Stanley Cavell and Yale's Harold Bloom, naturally from quite different directions. One thing these two strong readers hold in common, however, is the understanding that Emerson was and is to be taken seriously, that what he says about human life and fate is, in fact, necessary data. His great theme, the "infinitude of the private man," now properly rephrased as the infinite potential of the individual human consciousness, asserts that each person possesses in mind the equivalent powers that generate and sustain the universe. In effect, $e = mc^2$ is a human metaphor as well: Manifest power arises in consciousness and not just in mushroom clouds.

None of this capacity, however, yet manifests in contemporary religious and philosophical inquiry. In these environments we still stagger from the blows that scientific determinism has showered upon us. We have been told by these "reliable sources" that human beings are merely products of DNA's desire to create more DNA, that we are accidental by-products of genetic adaptation and mutation. Similarly, we're told, our *consciousness*—not just our brains!—has evolved from aeons of electrochemical reactions in the soup of the biosphere. We are expected to concede that matter has generated consciousness rather than the other way around.

Emerson tells me on every page that this is not so. He affirms that consciousness, the life of the mind, is part of an eternal consciousness, access to which each individual possesses. This primary fact is the place he found to "stand," following the famous Archimedes dictum: "Give me a place to stand and I will move the Earth." Emerson's understanding created a philosophical lever with its fulcrum beyond the confines of sensory perception. His very existence, he said, took its being from a source beyond our perceptions of nature, stars, and systems. His essential freedom and power (or leverage) came from this infinite Absolute, and from that stand he elected to participate.

Emerson's so-called Transcendent Idealism emerged refreshed and vibrant from a long strain of similar visions going all the way back to ancient Orphic mysteries. He is another Heraclitus, a solitary adversary to habit and banality, making assertions others would claim to be madness. He wrote and spoke for those who could hear his particular melody or strain of thought. It was not solely a matter of an elect or a special community of chosen believers. Who responded and who didn't was a mystery and always will be. He touched people according to their readiness to receive or their particular temperament. Often listeners or readers carried just one sentence away from a talk or reading, something that struck at their heart.

So many of these sentences have been preserved and held lovingly to heart by so many people through the years that literary critics of Emerson's work have spent time and energy examining these extraordinary pieces of grammar and syntax. What is it about them that moves us so? Consider these sentences, all in a sequence, from the magnificent essay "Circles:"

> There are no fixtures in nature. The universe is fluid and volatile. Permanence is but a word of degrees. Our globe seen by God is a transparent law, not a mass of facts. The law dissolves the fact and holds it fluid.

These are knives in the brain, cutting through the mess and general murky materialism of our ordinary perceptions. He says to us again and again: See! See! See!

How did he get there? What form of insight and inspiration results in sentences like these? Horatio might tell the Hamlet in us that it is to consider too closely to consider so, but we reply, "No, I want to know. Emerson asks me all the time not to follow him on his heels too closely, but rather to choose my own path, to achieve his level of self-reliance trusting my own thought. Yes, I want to know how to arrive there on my own."

The passage above from "Circles" could be from Heraclitus, the great philosopher from Ephesus in Asia Minor. Heraclitus spoke sentences like these and has been quoted for 2,500 years by all manner of people. Is it true, then, that voices like this, like father Heraclitus and his son Emerson, like Socrates and his son Plato, are destined to be solitary prophets crying in the desert? Does it mean that while they speak with inspiration in the wilderness of our souls the "civilized" world must perpetuate its ancient illusions and fanciful creeds?

I call this study of Emerson *God In Concord* because the Concord of 1833 to 1882 (the years Emerson lived there) was a time and a place of unique vision and importance to America. The title has a double intent. On one hand, it suggests that Emerson was interested in knowing God and in giving an accurate account of his inquiries into divine nature. On the other, it suggests that Emerson himself was, in a manner of speaking, a god in Concord. I mean this not in the sense of how he was regarded, but in the sense of how he embodied the divine principles he discovered.

Emerson was not alone in his visions, but he was clearly the best spokesman of them in his circle. He saw and proclaimed what he saw for everyone to hear and know. His published work is now very well known.

This study approaches the more private Emerson as recorded in his journals and notebooks, distinct from the well-known "Works." In his journals (sixteen volumes published by Harvard University from 1960 to 1982), we have his personal musings and early drafts of published work. We see his struggles as a writer, his personal reactions to those around him in life, illness, and death. We are present very near the moment of the revelations that emerged from the act of reflection taking place in his mind.

The center or starting point from which this text will spiral out is the famous "Divinity School Address," a sermon delivered by Emerson to a small group of students and their guests at Harvard College on the evening of July 15, 1838. The address so shocked the faculty of Divinity College that Emerson was effectively banned from formal Harvard functions for more than thirty years. Some still say it smacks of atheism. It is a story of the nobility of Boston society, the fathers of New England religious tradition, and a young ex-minister from Concord with a passion for the truth of reality.

*Divinity College Chapel, site of the "Address" delivered July 15, 1838*

# 1  CRISIS IN THE CHURCH

*On July 15, 1838,* Emerson traveled from his home in Concord to Cambridge to deliver his "Address" to the graduating class of Divinity College at Harvard. The six graduating students had invited Emerson, after talking with him about theism and the state of the Unitarian ministry some seven weeks earlier.

As this summer of Emerson's career began, few overtly negative declarations aimed at established religion had emerged in his lectures or published writing, even though a dozen years of journals were filled with them. His first small book, *Nature*, the ninety-page essay published in 1836, was not widely known, partly because it was so general. It would take twelve years to sell the first five hundred copies. In sharp contrast, three hundred copies of the address to the Divinity College students were printed late in August and sold out promptly. This one rattled the cages of the Unitarian clergy. Here was substantial controversy.

Something had finally pushed Emerson to the edge of heresy. As he prepared the "Address," he knew perfectly well what statements would bring strong reaction from the establishment; but even he would be shocked at the vehemence and volume of the cage-rattling that ensued. His appearance in Cambridge was, as he saw it, a perfect opportunity to develop his spiritual principles a step further and to challenge the banal, stultifying world of Unitarian preaching then current in eastern Massachusetts, particularly in Boston.

Several journal entries early in 1838 reveal the state of Emerson's mind and temperament. We begin with his thoughts about speaking to the students at Harvard:

1 APRIL. Cool or cold windy clear day. The Divinity School youths wished to talk with me concerning theism.[1] I went rather heavy-hearted for I always find that my views chill or shock people at the first opening, but the conversation went well & I came away cheered. I told them that the preacher should be a poet smit with love of the harmonies of moral nature: and yet look at the Unitarian Association & see if its aspect is poetic. They all smiled No. A minister nowadays is plainest prose, the prose of prose. He is a Warming-pan, a Night-chair at sick beds & rheumatic souls; and the fire of the minstrel's eye & the vivacity of his word is exchanged for intense grumbling enunciation of the Cambridge sort, & for scripture phraseology.[2]

Next, three weeks later, he reflected on his dreams:

20 APRIL. Last night, ill dreams. Dreams are true to nature & like monstrous formations (e.g. the horsehoof divided into toes) show the law. Their double consciousness, their sub- & ob-jectiveness is the wonder. I call the phantoms that rise the creation of my fancy but they act like volunteers & counteract my inclination. They make me feel that every act, every thought, every cause, is bipolar & in the act is contained the counteract. If I strike, I am struck. If I chase, I am pursued. If I push, I am resisted.[3]

Working on him through these weeks is an awareness, operating like a Platonic *daimon,* that he is approaching a series of strong assertions which will separate him permanently from his roots: from his tradition-bound Aunt Mary Moody, from his teachers at Harvard, and from some of his colleagues in the ministry. Three days later, he attends a meeting in Concord:

23 APRIL. Last night the old question of miracles was broached again at the Teachers' meeting & shown up & torn up in the usual manners. They think that God causes a miracle to make men. Stare & then says, Here is truth. They do not & will not perceive that it is to distrust the deity of truth—its invincible beauty—to do God a high dishonor,—so to depict him. They represent the old trumpery of God sending a messenger to raise man from his

low estate. Well then he must have credentials & miracle is the credentials. I answer God sends me messengers alway. I am surrounded by messengers of God who show me credentials day by day. Jesus is not a solitary but still a lovely herald.[4]

This clear difference in view of the nature of God—nature's daily miracles and the elevated state of human perception needed to glean the message—and this radical shift in theology will in three weeks be two themes of the address to the students. In these weeks Emerson begins to frame his argument. Before doing so, however, he first frames his temperament.

> JUNE 6. Every body, I think, has sublime thoughts sometimes. At times, they lie parallel with the world or the axes coincide so that you can see through them the great laws. *Then* be of their side. Let your influence be so true & simple as to bring them into these frames.[5]

This advice is as much to himself as it is to the students. The minister standing in the pulpit, looking down at upturned faces, is tempted to sow sublime thoughts, something like going straight for the answer before the question has been properly posed. In matters of God, planting doctrine dulls the mind. A sublime thought which lies parallel to the world in such a way as to reveal great laws cannot be tossed out over the pulpit in the "prose of prose" by a warming-pan. Still more in the journal that same day:

> Another thing. We resent all criticism which denies us any thing that lies in our line of advance. Say that I cannot paint a Transfiguration or build a steamboat, or be a grand marshal, & I shall not seem to me depreciated. But deny me any quality of metaphysical or literary power, & I am piqued. What does this mean? Why, simply that the soul has assurance by instincts & presentiments of *all* power in the direction of its ray, as well as the special skills it has already got.[6]

This brilliant observation, so crucial to later essays such as "Spiritual Laws," appears here as Emerson prepares his address. It is as though he feels the pique already in the objections his words will inevitably provoke, and he knows that very specific feeling marks the true path of his vision and the direction of his life. He will brook no opposition, but he will also not vent his anger in defense. Indeed, the next day he gives himself a warning about his reaction to criticism.

7 JUNE . . . Reserve your fire. Keep your temper. Render soft answers. Bear & forbear. Do not dream of suffering for ten years yet. Do not let the word *martyrdom* ever escape out of the white fence of your teeth.[7]

When July 15 finally arrived, the half-dozen students and their families, a few members of the faculty, and a few of Emerson's friends gathered in the small second-floor chapel in Divinity Hall.[8] What the small audience heard that evening was, to most, astonishing. So compact was the thought, so moving the affection poured out to the young men, and so radical the implications for Christianity as practiced in New England, that even today students at Harvard Divinity School should not be able to read the address without some religious turmoil. The issues, in other words, are still with us. No person preparing to enter the ministry can afford to ignore this sermon.

We know that the address was the culmination of impressions, thoughts, and ideas gathering in Emerson from age sixteen because in 1819, his junior year at Harvard College, he began to keep his journals. In them we follow the progression to this fateful day. Early on, when still an undergraduate, he had accepted the inevitability of becoming a minister, following a long family tradition of service to the Church. From then on—through his own studies at the Divinity School, through illness and near blindness, through marriage and the death of his first wife Ellen, through the resignation from his post at the Second Church in Boston, through travels in Europe, through his marriage to Lydia Jackson and the start of a new home and family in Concord, through these nearly twenty years—he recorded the thoughts and images which build to this day and provide his platform, his place to stand.

The "Address" is direct, vivid, and uncompromising. It differs from the diffuse power of *Nature* in those respects. It differs also from the social and scientific lecture series that occupied Emerson through much of the 1830s. It differs from his more traditional "American Scholar" address at Harvard the summer before, in which he prodded America's lagging independence from European cultural influence and set forth his vision of "Man Thinking." The "Address" literally breaks apart the carefully circumscribed confines of the human relationship to God, the identity and divinity of Jesus, and the fundamental purpose of human life.

In great measure the power of the "Address" comes from the sense of urgency Emerson felt, the crisis in the life of the New England Church. Even though in his own resignation six years before he had acted upon issues close to his own conscience, he also felt increasingly that the Church itself was in crisis, that Christianity in his era had lost its way. He had even begun to wonder why one should attend church at all. His journal entry in March, four months prior to the "Address," explores those feelings:

> At church all day but almost tempted to say I would go no more. Men go where they are wont to go else had no soul gone this afternoon. The snowstorm was real, the preacher merely spectral. Vast contrast to look at him & then out the window. Yet no fault in the good man. Evidently he thought himself a faithful searching preacher, mentioned that he thought so several times; & seemed to be one of that large class, *sincere persons based on shams; sincere persons who are bred & do live in shams.* He had lived in vain . . . I think it shows what I said on the last page to be true, that there is commanding attraction in the moral sentiment that can lend a faint tint of light to such dulness & ignorance as this coming in its place & name. What a cruel injustice it is to moral nature to be thus behooted & behowled, & not a law, not a word of it articulated.[9]

Only in the last section of this entry does Emerson see some glimmer of positive value for people to come together in the church setting. In fact, his last thought on the matter, further down the page is this: "The Church is a good place to study Theism by comparing the things said to your Consciousness," but there is little conviction in it. He reminds himself to busy himself in self-reflection while the sham is in progress. One is reminded of Galileo ignoring the service and discovering the laws of the pendulum while sitting in church.

What is the sham? The "Address" spells it out. First though, Emerson articulates the principles of the sentiment of virtue and the moral law upon which all true religion is founded. What he said may have seemed abstract and vague to some in the audience, but the message was clear enough and would have been familiar to most of the students.

> The intuition of the moral sentiment is an insight of the perfection of the laws of the soul. These laws execute themselves. They are out of time, out of space, and not subject to circumstance. Thus in the soul of man there is a justice whose retributions are instant and entire. He who does a good deed, is instantly ennobled. He who does a mean deed, is by the action itself contracted. He who puts off impurity, thereby puts on purity. If a man is at heart just, then in so far is he God; the safety of God, the immortality of God, the majesty of God do enter into that man with justice. If a man dissemble, deceive, he deceives himself, and goes out of acquaintance with his own being. A man in the view of absolute goodness, adores, with total humility. Every step so downward, is a step upward. The man who renounces himself, comes to himself.

Although there lies hidden in this passage an articulation of Emerson's Law of Compensation, which remains one of the most challenging of his ideas and one that will occupy us soon, the rest of the passage articulates a position comfortable to most listeners. Not even the scowling Andrews Norton could seriously object to the assertion that "if a man is at heart just, then in so far is he God." The phrase "in so far" would have placated the traditionalists. It is the classic idea of the imitation of Christ. Then, however, after the positive assertions of the sentiments of virtue and moral law, Emerson begins his attack:

> And because the indwelling Supreme Spirit cannot wholly be got rid of, the doctrine of it suffers this perversion, that the divine

nature is attributed to one or two persons, and denied to all the rest, and denied with fury.

The assertion that confining "divine nature" to Jesus and, one would assume from the previous passage, the Buddha, is a perversion of truth shows Emerson's aggressively positive method. In that previous paragraph he inclusively draws upon the beliefs of Eastern religions as proof of the wisdom of his position:

The sentences of the oldest time, which ejaculate this piety, are still fresh and fragrant. This thought dwelled always deepest in the minds of men in the devout and contemplative East; not alone in Palestine, where it reached its purest expression, but in Egypt, in Persia, in India, in China. Europe has always owed to oriental genius, its divine impulses. What these holy bards said, all sane men found agreeable and true.

The next step, after almost casually asserting that of the views so far stated "none will contest," Emerson points out two errors in the Christianity practiced in 1838.

Jesus Christ belonged to the true race of prophets. He saw with open eye the mystery of the soul. Drawn by its severe harmony, ravished with its beauty, he lived in it, and had his being there. Alone in all history, he estimated the greatness of man. One man was true to what is in you and me. He saw that God incarnates himself in man, and evermore goes forth anew to take possession of his world. He said, in this jubilee of sublime emotion, "I am divine. Through me, God acts; through me, speaks. Would you see God, see me; or, see thee, when thou also thinkest as I now think." But what a distortion did his doctrine and memory suffer in the same, in the next, and the following ages! There is no doctrine of the Reason which will bear to be taught by the Understanding. The understanding caught this high chant from the poet's lips, and said, in the next age, "This was Jehovah come down out of heaven. I will kill you, if you say he was a man." The idioms of his language, and the figures of his rhetoric, have usurped the place of his truth; and churches are not built on his principles, but on his tropes. Christianity became a Mythus, as the poetic teaching of Greece and of Egypt, before. He spoke of miracles; for he felt that man's life was a miracle, and all that man doth, and he knew that this daily miracle shines, as the character ascends. But the word Miracle, as pronounced by Christian churches, gives a false impression; it is Monster. It is not one with the blowing clover and the falling rain.

What is a Christian to do with this passage? Emerson feels free to offer an interpretation of the words of Jesus given as quotation, a very loose manipulation of text. Most ministers are more careful to work from holy writ and then offer an interpretation. Emerson the strong reader feels free to strongly rewrite: "I am divine. Through me, God acts; through me, speaks. Would you see God, see me; or, see thee, when thou also thinkest as I now think." What devout Christians do with this passage ultimately depends upon their own experience and some attention to Emerson's intent. In his important book *The American Religion,* Harold Bloom has this comment on Emerson's famous passage:

> Emerson, like William James after him, makes the American Religion beautifully overt, and after more than one hundred fifty years, this passage still has the capacity to give offence, particularly to Fundamentalists who cannot understand their own version of the American Religion. What makes Emerson's paragraph a superb model for American religious criticism is condensed into its key sentence: "The idioms of his language, and the figures of his rhetoric, have usurped the place of his truth; and churches are not built on his principles, but on his tropes." . . . Emerson knows that religion is imagined, and always must be reimagined.10

Emerson "reimagines" the teaching of Jesus in the crucible of his own spiritual experience. That language changes, is altered, indeed reimagined, should not surprise anyone aware of the transmission of text and the alterations of translation. Emerson's intent was well stated earlier in the sermon and cannot be mistaken. It is framed in his vision of the One Mind and his views on good and evil.

These facts have always suggested to man the sublime creed, that the world is not the product of manifold power, but of one will, of one mind; and that one mind is everywhere active, in each ray of the star, in each wavelet of the pool; and whatever opposes that will, is everywhere balked and baffled, because things are made so, and not otherwise. Good is positive. Evil is merely privative, not absolute: it is like cold, which is the privation of heat. All evil is so much death or nonentity. Benevolence is absolute and real. So much benevolence as a man hath, so much life hath he. For all things proceed out of this same spirit, which is differently named love, justice, temperance, in its different applications, just as the ocean receives different names on the several shores which it washes. All things proceed out of the same spirit, and all things conspire with it. Whilst a man seeks good ends, he is strong by the whole strength of nature.

The assertion that "evil is merely privative" and that only "benevolence is absolute and real" may strike the modern ear as naïve. After all, we have witnessed the evidences of evil incarnate, holocausts so malignant that we dare not offend such a force, we suppose, by denying its absolute existence. And yet Emerson's vision of unity hinges on the statement that "all things proceed out of the same spirit," and the nature of that spirit is pure benevolence. Evil is caused by ignorance, is privative, and ignorance is a function of separation and absence, as cold is the absence of heat.

As he went on to say in the "Address," however, "The good, by affinity, seek the good; the vile, by affinity, the vile. Thus of their own volition souls proceed into heaven, into hell." What may seem a contradiction here is none. Emerson saw heaven and hell as degrees in a spectrum of affinities. After death, the soul seeks its own nature. If our affinity is to the cold, so be it. Justice, then, is natural and proper linking of lawful affinities.

Emerson raises this issue because the received tradition of his time, emerging as it did from dualistic Puritan roots, saw Satan as absolute and real, a force in direct opposition to God's benevolence. If that formulation of evil is true, therefore, we can never trust our intuitions. We must depend, therefore, on higher authority. In order to trust our intuition, as Emerson wishes us to do, we have to be able to judge its authenticity directly through the fruits of love, justice, and temperance. In Emerson's philosophy everything rises from this assertion. He states it clearly:

> Meantime, whilst the doors of the temple stand open, night and day, before every man, and the oracles of this truth cease never, it is guarded by one stern condition; this, namely; it is an intuition. It cannot be received at second hand. Truly speaking, it is not instruction, but provocation, that I can receive from another soul. What he announces, I must find true in me, or wholly reject; and on his word, or as his second, be he who he may, I can accept nothing. On the contrary, the absence of this primary faith is the presence of degradation.

What follows are examples of the degradation in the preaching of the Christian message:

> . . . Historical Christianity has fallen into the error that corrupts all attempts to communicate religion. As it appears to us, and as it has appeared for ages, it is not the doctrine of the soul, but an exaggeration of the personal, the positive, the ritual. It has dwelt, it dwells, with noxious exaggeration about the "*person*" of Jesus. The soul knows no persons. It invites every man to expand to the full circle of the universe, and will have no preferences but those of spontaneous love. But by this eastern monarchy of a Christianity, which indolence and fear have built, the friend of man is made the injurer of man. The manner in which his name is surrounded with expressions, which were once sallies of admiration and love, but are now petrified into official titles, kills all generous sympathy and liking.

Jesus is pictured here not as Savior but as Destroyer, reducing human beings to abject idol-worshippers, seeking the shade of Apollo in the ruins of Delphi. Emerson's charge would not have elicited such virulent reaction had it ended here even with its images of petrified preaching or of churches paralyzed by banality. But Emerson is only beginning. The implications of idol worship have their effect on the meaning of human life:

> You shall not own the world; you shall not dare, and live after the infinite Law that is in you, and in company with the infinite Beauty which heaven and earth reflect to you in all lovely forms; but you must subordinate your nature to Christ's nature; you must accept our interpretations; and take his portrait as the vulgar draw it.

Here is the crux. Elevate Jesus and diminish yourself, and then accept the implications: beating your breast and your head against the wall of sin; fearing the eternal fires of Hell and the wrath of God; being subservient. What are you anyway? Just a human being. Nothing but a rational animal confined to the dust and ooze of evolution, just a mass of DNA coming apart at the genes. Or, as Emerson put it: "A pagan, suckled in a creed outworn."

Emerson's next attack was aimed at the nature of revelation itself. It is not enough that we make an idol of Jesus, but we also stop the flow of God's Word and confine it to the received tradition guarded by Authority.

> The second defect of the traditionary and limited way of using the mind of Christ is a consequence of the first; this, namely; that the Moral Nature, that Law of laws, whose revelations introduce greatness,—yea, God himself, into the open soul, is not explored as the fountain of the established teaching in society. Men have come to speak of the revelation as somewhat long ago given and done, as if God were dead. The injury to faith throttles the preacher; and the goodliest of institutions becomes an uncertain and inarticulate voice.

What is the good of preaching at all if we are restricted to what has been said before? Indeed, so-called Born Again Fundamentalist sects are growing abundantly in America today precisely because of the freedom preachers feel to interpret sacred text in the light of their parishioners' immediate personal needs. That errors are made in extracting meaning from text is a given and is not important. The test, in any case, is not the authority of experts but rather the degree to which the immediate spiritual needs of people are met. In the great supermarket of religion, people buy what attracts them as they pass down the aisles.

What has been abandoned in charismatic environments where the fruits of the spirit are free to express themselves[11] is the influence of any external authority. What kills the spirit eventually in such environments is internal bureaucracy, the inevitable imposition of procedures on the spontaneous intuitions of the spirit, or "the open soul" as Emerson phrased it. Inevitably, when bureaucratic impulses overwhelm freedom of expression, thus inhibiting the free flow of the spirit, either the church atrophies or a schism occurs and a new community of worshippers is created, only to go through the same process. Even in the modern Quaker meeting, for example, where free expression of the Holy Spirit is given ample room, limits based on decorous behavior impose themselves and inhibition grows. Emerson himself was drawn to George Fox and the Quakers because their forms of worship came closest to his ideal community of the faithful. Nonetheless, given the inherent weaknesses of formal worship, he would agonize all his life over the issue of gathering for the worship of God.

At the end of the "Address," Emerson backs away from a call to rid the culture of formal worship in churches or to establish new forms. His solution for the present crisis lies in the youth and vision of these new preachers as they take their place in the established forms of worship.

> And now let us do what we can to rekindle the smouldering, nigh quenched fire on the altar. The evils of the church that now is are manifest. The question returns, What shall we do? I confess, all attempts to project and establish a Cultus with new rites and forms, seem to me vain. Faith makes us, and not we it, and faith makes its own forms. All attempts to contrive a system are as cold as the new worship introduced by the French to the goddess of Reason,— to-day, pasteboard and filigree, and ending to-morrow in madness and murder. Rather let the breath of new life be breathed by you

through the forms already existing. For, if once you are alive, you shall find they shall become plastic and new. The remedy to their deformity is, first, soul, and second, soul, and evermore, soul.

"Faith makes its own forms." Places of worship will always establish themselves, where like people come together to share like expressions of faith. The history of religion in America, where fresh impulses are encouraged and constitutionally guaranteed, illustrates Emerson's point. The Unitarians grew out of the Episcopal tradition in 1796, were joined by Congregational churches throughout New England, formed the Unitarian Association in 1825, and a century and a half later (in 1961) joined forces with the Universalist Association. Such a move would not have surprised Emerson, even in 1836, when he made the following observation about sectarian differences:

> There would be no sect if there were no Sect. Is this a foolish identical proposition? I mean that the reason why the Universalist appears is because something has been overstated or omitted by the antecedent sect and the human mind feels itself wronged and overstates on the other side as in this. Each of our sects is an extreme statement & therefore obnoxious to contradiction & reproof. But each rests on this strong but obscure instinct of an outraged truth.[12]

Speaking with Unitarians in our own time, one still finds "outraged truth" in Emerson's statements concerning the exclusive divinity of Jesus Christ. The sectarian differences that persist reflect growing acceptance of individual convictions within sects, differences not tolerated in the New England sect of 1838. Indeed, as we look more carefully at the responses to the "Address," the more we recognize the real motive behind the attacks immediately following its first presentation.

As mentioned earlier, members of the faculty of the School of Divinity were in the front pews of the chapel on July 15, 1838. Among them was Andrews Norton, a faculty member from 1819 to 1830. In his retirement Norton was working on a three-volume study of *The Evidences of the Genuineness of the Gospels*, published in parts in 1837 and 1844. Norton's formal response to Emerson's "Address" was the most virulent of the many criticisms published. In a letter to *The Boston Daily Advertiser*, August 27, 1838, Norton scattered his shot broadly, aiming in general at all transcendental thinking and then closing in point blank on Emerson in particular:

> The rejection of reasoning is accompanied with an equal contempt for good taste. All modesty is laid aside. The writer of an article for an obscure periodical, or a religious newspaper, assumes a tone as if he were one of the chosen enlighteners of a dark age. —He continually obtrudes himself upon his reader, and announces his own convictions, as if from having that character, they were necessarily indisputable . . .

Early in the letter Norton accuses Emerson and his transcendental cohorts of abandoning reason in their zeal to put forward their radical views. Norton himself, however, abandons reason as the level of his invective rises. He directs readers' attention to the evil in their midst:

> The evil is becoming, for the time disastrous and alarming; and of this fact there could hardly be a more extraordinary and ill boding evidence, than is afforded by a publication, which has just appeared, entitled, an "Address, delivered before the Senior Class in Divinity College, Cambridge, . . . by Ralph Waldo Emerson."
>
> It is not necessary to remark particularly on this composition. It will be sufficient to state generally, that the author professes to reject all belief in Christianity as a revelation, that he makes a general attack upon the Clergy, on the ground that they preach what he calls "Historical Christianity."

What comes next exposes Norton's real motive in writing in opposition to Emerson's views: his deep distress at the challenge of Authority, he himself representing the fundamental hierarchy of Christian truth and teaching, both at Harvard and the Divinity College.

> . . . the main question is how it has happened, that religion has been insulted by the delivery of these opinions in the Chapel of the Divinity College of Cambridge, as the last instruction which those were to receive, who were going forth from it, bearing the name of Christian preachers. This is a question in which the com-

munity is deeply interested. No one can doubt for a moment of the disgust and strong disapprobation with which it must have been heard by the highly respectable officers of that Institution. They must have felt it not only as an insult to religion, but as personal insult to themselves. But this renders the fact of its having been so delivered only the more remarkable. We can proceed but a step in accounting for it. The preacher was invited to occupy the place he did, not by the officers of the Divinity College, but by the members of the graduating class. These gentleman, therefore, have become accessories, perhaps innocent accessories, to the commission of a great offence; and the public must be desirous of learning what exculpation or excuse they can offer.

Here is a tense, vindictive, and personal attack aimed at Emerson the man. The letter never engages the religious issues presented by Emerson.

We know that Norton was probably predisposed to personal animosity. He had observed Emerson's unorthodox studies at Divinity College a decade before. Emerson had been prevented by near blindness from pursuing normal studies and had, instead, prepared himself for formal approbation into the ministry almost exclusively on his own. His taste in reading during this period had been eclectic, not at all devoted to the standard texts of divinity training.

Norton could have known nothing of Emerson's intellectual or spiritual pursuits. All that Norton knew at the time was that, in his view, this particular student had neither fulfilled the expected requirements nor demonstrated mastery of logical argument or scholarly discipline. Therefore, when the invitation had been extended, not by the faculty, but rather by the graduating class of the College, Norton was predisposed to respond critically.

The vituperation of the response, however, goes well beyond mere criticism of content or disapproval of a choice of speaker. Norton saw in Emerson a power which if not checked would be a genuine threat to the authority of the Church. The passion of this address told Norton that here was a Satanic force let loose in the sanctuary.[13] Harvard itself was under attack, he thought; and unless this force were blunted now, the plague would spread and Christianity as a whole would be threatened. Also under attack in Norton's view was the social order in Boston and Cambridge, of which Norton was one of the pillars. His patriarchal and hierarchal sense of stability, created and sustained by education and respect for authority, was being challenged by this upstart from Concord—a person known by the normative community to be unstable as one who had resigned an important position at the famed Second Church, a person whose family was outside the well-established social strata of Boston society by virtue of their poverty if not by their hereditary claim to distinction.[14]

Two days after the address, Emerson made the following personal observation in his journal:

> [JULY] 17. In preparing to go to Cambridge with my speech to the young men, day before yesterday, it occurred to me with force that I had no right to go unless I were equally willing to be prevented from going.[15]

He had felt the importance of this occasion and had here, in one of his typical self-reflective moments, reached an understanding with himself about the nature of anticipation and its close relation to egotism. The thought is very Platonic, a Socrates-like sense of inaction and passive acceptance in the face of high moment. Giving himself this necessary detachment helped him to approach the address with equanimity.

The observation also illustrates Emerson's sense of the importance of this moment in his life. He did anticipate, greatly anticipate, this opportunity. It was historic, even if the circumstances appeared modest: the little chapel, the tiny class, the small audience. And yet, here he was in front of the Divinity College faculty, at Harvard, officially sanctioned, at least by the graduates, to speak his mind. Did he pull his punches? Was he awed into compromise by the occasion?

We think of the personal journal as a private place where we can speak our minds without fear of being shocking or misunderstood. In Emerson's case, at least in doctrinal or metaphysical matters, the journals serve to clarify or dramatize his formal writing, while only occasionally providing uncensored thoughts. Two weeks prior to the address, presumably while it was being written—in part using material from much earlier journal entries—he penned the following in late June:

Most of the Commonplaces spoken in churches every Sunday respecting the Bible & the life of Christ, are grossly superstitious. Would not, for example, would not any person unacquainted with the bible, always draw from the pulpit the impression that the New Testament unfolded a system? and in the second place that the history of the life & teachings of Jesus were greatly more copious than they are? Do let the new generation speak the truth, & let the grandfathers die. Let go if you please the old notions about responsibility for the souls of your parishioners but do feel that Sunday is their only time for thought & do not defraud them of that, as miserably as two men have me today. Our time is worth too much than that we can go to church twice, until you have got something to announce there.[16]

Notions about the responsibility for the souls of one's parishioners strike at the heart of Norton's criticisms. The so-called "grandfathers" did feel this responsibility deeply. They were the shepherds with innocent flocks too easily led astray by the temptations of this world. Their task, as they were taught to see it, was to protect, warn, and console. The preacher administered to life's passages: birth, baptism, religious training, marriage, crisis, and death. Beyond these boundaries, a preacher was not to trespass.

Emerson, on the other hand, was willing to trust that the individual with his or her own soul at stake will take the moral path once given the gift of reflective thought. Conscience is the key, and while it sleeps within, the individual is vulnerable to the pressures of the world. To awaken that conscience, sleeping within the recesses of the soul/mind, is what Emerson saw as the proper task of the preacher. All conversation, all formal sermonizing, should have as their goal the awakening of that self-reflective faculty.

At the close of the "Address," where Emerson reaches the formal

charge for the young graduates, he finds language so original and feelings so personal that they create the vision he so earnestly seeks to
convey. It is no wonder that the "grandfathers" present could make no
sense of it. They had no personal experience with it.

> Yourself a newborn bard of the Holy Ghost,—cast behind you all
> conformity, and acquaint men at first hand with Deity. Look to it
> first and only, that fashion, custom, authority, pleasure, and money,
> are nothing to you,—are not bandages over your eyes, that you
> cannot see,—but live with the privilege of the immeasurable mind.
> Not too anxious to visit periodically all families and each family
> in your parish connection,—when you meet one of these men or
> women, be to them a divine man; be to them thought and virtue;
> let their timid aspirations find in you a friend; let their trampled
> instincts be genially tempted out in your atmosphere; let their
> doubts know that you have doubted, and their wonder feel that
> you have wondered. By trusting your own heart, you shall gain
> more confidence in other men. For all our penny-wisdom, for all
> our soul-destroying slavery to habit, it is not to be doubted, that
> all men have sublime thoughts; that all men value the few real
> hours of life; they love to be heard; they love to be caught up into
> the vision of principles.

How many preachers or teachers of any stripe have we encountered
who have the vision and/or the capacity to approach their charges in
such as way as to let culturally trampled instincts be genially tempted
out in the atmosphere of their church or classroom? First, one has to
have a sense of what "trampled instincts" might be and, second, by
what process they may be "tempted out" in the right atmosphere. Certainly Emerson knew full well how difficult these matters are to
understand for those who have never seen the human being in this
light, and he would devote the next twenty years to both concepts.

That few professionals in the field of religion understood Emerson
was obvious from the reactions over the next six months. It wasn't so
much that theologians or ministers took the philosophical tenets of
Emerson's gnostic vision and opposed it *per se.* They simply attacked

Emerson personally or else accused him of importing vile foreign (French and German) thinking into the sanctuary of English-speaking reason and tradition.

The most dramatic of these reactions came from three members of the faculty of the Theological Seminary at Princeton. J.W. Alexander, Albert Dod, and Charles Hodge issued a response to the "Address" in *The Biblical Repertory and Princeton Review* for January, 1839. Again, what was issued was not a theological document in terms of reasoned discourse; it was a diatribe against "the nonsense and impiety" of the "new" thinking.

When Emerson asserted in the "Address" that religious truth is an intuition which can not be received at second hand, he immediately offended most teachers of theology. How else, they might have wondered, can I teach the truths of Christianity without making them the objects of instruction? Teachers unable to answer that question satisfactorily could never tempt out trampled instincts in any atmosphere. Like the officials in Cambridge, the faculty of Princeton bristled.

> We pretend not, as we said, to comprehend these dogmas. We know not what they are; but we know what they are *not*. . . . No one, who has ever heard such avowals, can forget the touching manner in which pious as well as celebrated German scholars have sometimes lamented their still lingering doubts as to the personality of God. But while these systems rob us of our religious faith, they despoil us of our reason. Let those who will, rehearse to us the empty babble about reason as a faculty of immediate insight of the infinite; we will trust no faculty, which, like Eastern princes, mounts the throne over the corpses of its brethren. We cannot sacrifice our understanding. If we are addressed by appeals to consciousness, to intuition, we will try those appeals. If we are addressed by reasoning, we will endeavour to go along with that reasoning. But in what is thus offered, there is no ratiocination; there is endless assertion, not merely of unproved, but of unreasonable, of contradictory, of absurd propositions. And if any overcome by the *prestige* of

the new philosophy, as transatlantic, or as new, are ready to repeat dogmas which neither they, nor the inventors of them, can comprehend, and which approach the dialect of Bedlam, we crave to be exempt from the number, and will contentedly abstain for life from "the high *priory* road." The more we have looked at it, the more we have been convinced of its emptiness and fatuity. It proves nothing; it determines nothing; or, where it seems to have results, they are hideous and godless.[17]

Where Emerson was vulnerable in this "appraisal" is in the absence of "ratiocination," or the faculty in the intellect of discursive reasoning. By asserting the primacy of intuition, he could not very well turn his back on its revelations and argue discursively in explanation of his insights. To so would effectively cancel out the one in the syntax of the other. As he said in "Experience" about just persons, "They refuse to explain themselves, and are content that new actions should do them that office." In his scholarly case, the new actions would be in the form of new expression, new intuitions.

The key to Emersonian syntax was trust in the incisive observation, incisively expressed. Any interpolation that had the feel of explanation about it diminished its truth as much as it weakened the impact. Most famously from "Self-Reliance": "Nothing is sacred but the integrity of your own mind." Adding explanation to that thought in the form of definitions or examples removes its integrating power. Every attempt to amplify it reduces it and is the bane of all Emerson critics, the author included. The proper approach to Emerson is always amplification rather than explanation. What wanted amplification for the men of Princeton was the nature and authority of Emerson's revelations. That they referred generally to the content of the address as just so much "German insanity" showed their unwillingness to address the issues, much less recognize from what spiritual country the messenger had arrived in their midst. All they knew was that he wasn't from England.

# 2 THE GERMAN INSANITY

*In the final* paragraph of their diatribe against Emerson's "Address," the trio in Princeton make reference to Socinianism and what they call "the German insanity." They sum up their objections as follows:

> . . . the tendency of German philosophizing is towards impious temerity. We have long deplored the spread of Socinianism, but there is no form of Socinianism, or of rational Deism, which is not immeasurably to be preferred to the German insanity.[1]

Socinianism was a religious movement that spread west from Poland after 1605. It rejected the Nicene creed and adhered to the humanity of Jesus. In effect, it was an important influence on Unitarianism. The Princeton Trinitarians, although rejecting the Unitarian "heresy," nonetheless preferred it to the so-called German insanity. In their view, any dependence on the human mind as a reliable source of spiritual knowledge was insanity and marked the believer as a resident of Bedlam.

This schism in America during the 1830s and 1840s was as important to the development of a national spiritual psyche as is the current conflict between Traditionalism and Fundamentalism in American Christianity. The arguments in Emerson's time have a bearing on our own debate in the struggle between individually conceived and received religious belief in the Protestant tradition and a hierarchal, authoritarian conformism.

In Emerson's time, the debate among educated readers began with Kant's response to Locke's "Essay on Human Understanding" and to the opposing skepticism of Hume. Locke's great essay had been printed in 1690 and was the clearest expression to date of the authority of the human mind to explore the reality and limits of human experience. Hume, on the other hand, asserted that since all knowledge came from experience, the mind could not truly "know" anything on its own. Kant's brilliant essays came nearly one hundred years later, in the 1780s. They carried the discussion into the deep abyss between Locke and Hume and into the depths of the mysteries of consciousness, revealing aspects of intuition, understanding, and reason never before exposed to such rigorous philosophical examination.

Aside from his impact on the study of philosophy—which was, of course, immense—Kant's contribution to religious debate was to sanction the human mind as a perceiver of objective, *a priori*, knowledge. Although Kant stopped short of affirming that finite or objective spiritual knowledge could emerge from subjective understanding, he did open the doors to more adventuresome scholars who sought to lengthen his shadow into the infinite. The most important of these scholars in Emerson's time were Fichte, Jacobi, Goethe, and Novalis, interpretations of whose thinking came to America from England mostly through the English filter of Thomas Carlyle. These thinkers, working through and beyond Kant, established the speculative mind as a viable opposing source of knowledge in the philosophical debate with objective experience.

One can even argue that a philosophy of mind as an *a priori* source of subjective spiritual knowledge replaced medieval scholasticism as the effort to bring reason and faith into a coherent unity. Nonetheless, we still see today the vestiges of the scholastic system paraded through St. Peter's Square in the robes and rituals of Roman Catholicism. Even Pope John Paul II's late (October, 1996) recognition of scientific evolution is an example of scholastic system-building, and is therefore not a true synthesis of reason and faith in the Kantian sense.

For the German revisionists of the nineteenth century, however, speculation had already dismissed the ancient faith in divine revelation within sacred texts. The monumental work of Johann Gottfried Eichhorn (1752–1827) at Gottengen systematically removed the biblical texts from their sacrosanct immunity from scholarly investigation. (Emerson's older brother William sailed from Boston in December, 1823, took up study in Germany, and came under the influence of Eichhorn. His letters back to Waldo recommended the great critical works of Eichhorn to his attention.) It was a testament to Eichhorn's personal demeanor and assiduous scholarship that even the conservatives of the Theological Seminary at Princeton were hard pressed to find fault with the great man's work.

What prompted the divines of Princeton to the term "insanity," then, was not Eichhorn but rather the works of two of Kant's disciples, Jacobi and Fichte, both of whom took their master's work beyond his own carefully proscribed boundaries. Frederick Jacobi developed what has been called "Faith Philosophy," the basis of which is that once intuition is recognized as primary and no longer subservient to the understanding, the promptings of intuition can be authentic, or objectively existing. The obvious fault in Jacobi's view is the impossibility of determining the validity in each case of the private intuition. As we shall see, this is a problem which would occupy Emerson in all of his writings.

For Johann Fichte (1762–1814) the issue was not one of moving beyond the carefully defined limits of Kant's thinking into untenable territory, but rather of extending the implications of Kantian thought into spiritual areas. Fichte was larger than life, a heroic figure of Romantic leanings who regarded Kant's rigor as the anchor for his own admittedly undisciplined imagination. Fichte was a strong writer, which was an attraction for Emerson, one who described human consciousness in terms worthy of its true range and power. If the world exists, Fichte said, we know that fact through consciousness, which is creative, powerful, and primary: The essential fact of the universe is first and foremost consciousness. This position, in which God is an extension of fundamental consciousness but not necessarily its original creator, is what prompted the accusation of German insanity and the charge of *de facto* atheism.

The charge of supreme egoism leveled at both Jacobi and Fichte cannot be summarily dismissed. We see the same influence much later in Nietzsche, who was a devoted student of Emerson's work, but who turned away from its spiritual assertions and, later, became a

tragic victim of insanity. In all these cases, the vast power released by
the individual mind, seen by these thinkers as innate within the human
being, proved one way or another too much for their temperaments.
Emerson would solve this very real problem by seeing the immense
powers of consciousness residing *outside* the individual as something
like a stream of power into which we tap, like stepping down high-ten-
sion power lines for ordinary household use. Without some way of
transforming the power, we would blow our circuits, especially when
we are dealing with spiritual power.

Once we accept the idea of consciousness as a powerful supreme
reality, somehow beyond ourselves yet *here,* we then have to look at the
world and ask in what context and in what way the world exists as an
expression of that consciousness. What is the stuff of the universe? For
example, let us consider one of the objections to Emerson's "Address"
raised by the Princeton article. It was aimed at the concluding passage
where Emerson said:

> I look for the new Teacher, that shall follow so far those shining
> laws, that he shall see them come full circle; shall see their round-
> ing complete grace; shall see the world to be the mirror of the soul;
> shall see the identity of the law of gravitation with purity of heart;
> and shall show that the Ought, that Duty, is one thing with Sci-
> ence, with Beauty, and with Joy.

In the traditional religious view, we will never see the "identity of
the law of gravitation with purity of heart." Emerson's great thesis is
that we are one with the laws of the universe. Purity of heart is what
maintains our proper orbit. The limitations of human experience seen
as gravitation on the level of nature are in fact the laws of the soul.
That Emerson could see Duty and Joy as both an expression of our
duality and potential unity showed the range of his vision. That he
expressed duality in such imagery showed his instincts as a writer and
thinker. His ambition was to bring that vision and expression into
expressions of unity.

In the process, however, he courted a great danger. As Irving Howe
has pointed out in *The American Newness,*[2] Emerson knew perfectly

well that he did not wish to humanize religion—that is, to remove it from its divine source and place its precepts and values solely in the human arena. He didn't intend to take compassion, charity, love, and devotion and place them into some cultural context, creating a humanistic religion of community. He did not want to be a homogenized Jesus, wandering the streets of Concord doing good deeds and setting the example for the populace. Alcott was enough of a local saint. Concord didn't need another.

Emerson's investigations, based as they were on daily experience filtered through the lens of reflective thought, would always hold God as the divine ground beyond human comprehension. Because he refused to humanize the religious experience, as William James did in his role as a religious pragmatist, some twentieth-century intellectuals refer to Emerson as fatuous. They say he showed a blatant disregard for reality and proposed ludicrous visions in the place of common sense.[3] Indeed, to people who see God and religion as "dead issues," any attempt to create meaningful metaphors for their reality must seem fatuous.

What I argue in this text is that Emerson took it upon himself to create viable metaphors of their reality. From his experience and from the intuitions of his creative talent as a writer, he pursued a vision and crafted a language of the human relation to and movement toward transcendent divinity. Emerson meant what he said about this vision and this movement.

From the philosophical perspective, meaning what we say is a complex, challenging discipline, as Stanley Cavell explored in his series of essays, *Must We Mean What We Say?*[4] In the foreword to the essays, Cavell says, "Meaning what one says becomes a matter of making one's sense present to oneself."[5] This is an apt description of Emerson's method. Cavell goes on to explain why Wittgenstein described his own later philosophy as an effort "to bring words back to everyday use": philosophical discussion, as well as religious discussion, has been "away." We listen to the words and perceive them as foreign to our experience. "Away" can also mean "irrelevant," in the sense of not being coincident with our experience.

Cavell makes another important and useful reference to Wittgenstein in relation to Kant, this one concerning the relationship of language to knowledge. When Emerson proposed answers to philosophical and theological questions, he framed his answers in unique bursts of assertion or information in a certain grammar. Cavell, speaking of "matters of fact," says, "It is a language of what Wittgenstein means by grammar—the same thing as the knowledge Kant calls 'transcendental'."[6] As Emerson knew, the word "transcendental" was defined by Kant as signifying "such knowledge as concerns the *a priori* possibility of knowledge, or its *a priori* employment."[7]

Emerson's assertions arise from an internal dialogue between imagination and intuition, and they burst onto the page as metaphoric approximations of his intensely observed experience. To this extent, Emerson never argues a point, nor does he address both sides of an issue in formal argument. He takes issue with another's point of view only to refine a fact or point out an excess, as in the case of his essays on Swedenborg, Goethe, and Plato. Therefore, Emerson's "grammar" is his transcendental meaning.

While on the subject of Cavell and the language of philosophical inquiry, it is instructive to note a similarity observed in one of Cavell's essays, between some of Kierkegaard's concerns as they coincide with Emerson's. In the 1840s, when Emerson was at the peak of his expressive powers, Kierkegaard was writing essays arising from the travails of a minister named Adler whose claims to having had a revelation were being formally challenged by the Church. For Kierkegaard the question was, "How far may a man in our age be justified in asserting that he has had a revelation?"[8] This question will occupy us as we reach the point at which it becomes relevant to Emerson's grammar.

Cavell's interest cannot be whether or not an individual may have *had* a revelation, but rather whether we are in a position conceptually *to call* any pronouncement a revelation, given its traditional meaning and implications. Emerson never undertook to deal directly with this question, assuming as he always did the fact of revelatory experience at some level. It is, however, incumbent upon his readers, particularly in our time, to address the question as a primary issue in evaluating his impact and importance—especially as it was such an issue for his critics at the time. Although Emerson has found a secure place in the canon of American literature (and thus the American cultural experience), his position as a theologian and philosopher remains suspect. That tenuous position relates at least in part to the question of revelation and the individual's internal and external relationship to divinity.

The issue for us is very different from the concerns the theologians at Princeton expressed in 1838. Their intention was to rein in the excesses of "the German insanity" and to affirm the sanctity of biblical revelation as the sole source of God's law and will. Our concern is to evaluate Emerson's "grammar" (his transcendental assertions) in the light of his search for God and the nature of God's presence in human life. Is there God? Is God what we call a *personal* God? Or is the word "God" merely a symbol for self-regulating cosmic laws? In the light of these questions, what is prayer? To whom or what is prayer addressed?

These are Emerson's questions, and it is surprising how pervasive is scholars' neglect of them in evaluating his work. To regard Emerson as an inspirational essayist, a humanist, a provider of solace in the dark hours of life, is, as we say, well and good; but these concerns are not his primary concerns. He was, by his own assertion, "an endless seeker with no past at my back." To take him at his word, and by "at his word" we mean within and because of his actual words, we must pursue his language to that end and no other. As a seeker, Emerson sought to express what it means to be a human being and, given that, how we are to conduct our lives.

What the divines at Princeton could not do was to acknowledge that Emerson was following a well-established tradition of pushing the limits of human perception a few more paces into the darkness. Their position was similar to those bureaucrats at the close of the nineteenth century who, in the service of saving money, urged the closing of the patent office because we had reached the logical end of invention. Our present climate, on the other hand, is its opposite, at least in spiritual terms. We find ourselves now in a land of channeled spirits, dream revelations, visions, omens, and prognosticators; in other words, millennial madness. It might be useful to have a patent office for religions!

Emerson understood that if he was to affirm the sanctity of intuitive revelation, he had to anchor his affirmations in the granite of New
England practicality. The nineteenth century in England, Continental
Europe, and America outside the academy was a hotbed of Spiritualism, Mesmerism, magic, astrology, Hermeticism, Animal Magnetism,
and assorted phenomena of all sorts.[9] All these interests fall into the
category of spiritual materialism. Philosophically an idealist, Emerson
regarded these phenomena as a low curiosity, as he called it. In his later
years, when Spiritualism was making serious headway among lecture
audiences and well-to-do homes in Boston, Emerson added a lecture
entitled "Demonology" to his repertoire. This journal entry in 1856
reflects his life-long attitude:

> There are many things of which a wise man would wish to be igno-
> rant, and this is one of them. Shun them, as you would shun the
> secrets of the undertaker, of the butcher, the secrets of the jakes &
> the dead-cart. The adepts are they who have mistaken flatulence,
> for inspiration. If this drivel which they report as the voice of spir-
> its were really such, we must find out a more decisive suicide.[10]

The choice of imagery may seem severe, but the stakes are high.
Emerson wants to be right. His high aim is to reveal the truth, and he
has no interest in whether or not the ghost of Franklin can be invoked
in someone's parlor. His interest is in the laws of the mind as they
exhibit the laws of the universe. That these two manifestations are one
he had no doubt, and the wise path to that truth is through a balanced
mind, no matter how much others might regard his as unbalanced.

Harold Bloom points out that Emerson is, in Henry James, Sr.'s
phrase, a man without a handle.[11] He is, philosophically speaking, slippery. Eschewing labels of any kind, Emerson's instinct led him to the
conviction that to name the phenomena is to kill it. His refusal to
debate or explain maintained a purity of expression. His unwillingness
to engage gave the opposition the illusion of easy victories and gave
Emerson private bouts of uncertainty and even depression, but he
stayed true to his silence. He was, to his audiences, like the composer
who, when asked the meaning of an étude, said, "Listen, I will play it
again."

What Emerson began to suspect was that the true path to spiritual reality lay in and through the structure and faculties of the human mind. To that end, he had no interest in doctrinal debates. The Trinitarians and Unitarians could nitpick all they wanted. He would focus on the essentials.

*Writing chair in Old Mance, Concord,*
*used by Emerson to work on Nature*

# 3    SEARCHING FOR MIND

*From his first* journal entries Emerson began making connections between mind, language, meaning, and experience. As already mentioned, he started keeping his journals in January, 1820, when he was sixteen and a junior at Harvard. The very first youthful philosophical reference to mind in the journals, in what he entitled Wide World 2, dated March 14, 1821, is to his reading of the Welsh philosopher Richard Price (1723–1791).

> I am reading Price on Morals & intend to read it with care & commentary. I shall set down here what remarks occur to me upon the matter or manner of his argument. On the 56 Page Dr. Price says that right & wrong are not determined by reasoning or deduction but by an ultimate perception of the human mind. It is to be desired that this were capable of satisfactory proof but as it is in direct opposition to the skeptical philosophy it cannot stand unsupported by strong and sufficient evidence. I will read more & see if it is proved or no. —He saith that the Understanding is this ultimate determiner.[1]

First, it is worth remembering that this entry comes from a seventeen year-old, somewhat explaining the need to affirm at the outset his future study and attention to the task. In fact, the young scholar did indeed, as we shall see, read with "care and commentary" in subsequent entries.

The editors of the journals point out that Emerson quotes Price incorrectly in a key passage. Where Emerson, referring to the perception of right and wrong, uses the phrase "by an ultimate perception of the human mind," Price actually used the phrase "by some immediate power of perception in the human mind." Throughout his life Emerson tended to quote to his own understanding rather than copying out exactly from a text he was studying. Here he was obviously rendering a sense of authentic source in "immediate" rather than immediate in time.

Emerson's choice of quotation from Price here is an early indication of his interest in authenticating intuitive processes. He is also interested in proof of this elusive claim by Price. Later, he comes back to the matter.

> Dr. Price wrote to prove that the Understanding judges in questions of moral rectitude and has proved himself one of the ablest champions of truth . . .

On the next page of his journal Emerson meditates on the problem of determining the will of God:

> In ascertaining the will of the Deity it does not always proceed on the principle that the greatest happiness is intended, for this we cannot know, it is judged safer therefore to reason from adaptation and analogy. The moral sense/faculty or as others term it the decision of the understanding[2] is recognized as an Original principle of our nature, the *intuition* [emphasis Emerson's] by which we directly determine the merit or demerit of an action.[3]

These three passages in which Price takes a role illustrate the way the young Emerson found points of intersection with his own insights and adapted them to his own reflection on a topic. The passages also illustrate his growing interest in matters of the structure of Mind and the link between the interactions of Understanding and Intuition.

Over the next four years in particular, Emerson would seek out the images of intersection between the human and Divine Mind. Properly, he came to the search initially from a position of pure faith, a fundamental belief in the existence of God, in whatever nature that might be. This is entirely in keeping with what we see in the *Fides Quarens Intellectum,* that any serious exploration into the realm of Divine presence must proceed from a position of faith. Even Hume points out that any skepticism in this regard necessarily blocks an experience of the realm. The seeker must proceed with an inquiry having as its focus the principle, "Ask and you will receive," rather than "Prove to me, Lord, that you are there."

More problematic for Emerson in the early stages of his development was the nature and capacity of the human mind and its capacity to enter into the abyss of consciousness to make contact with the Divine Mind. Much later, in "Illusions," he would say: "The intellect is stimulated by the statement of truth in a trope." This oblique means of perception would suffice for him in receiving intimations of God.

But to return to beginnings, the first journal entry in this search is contained in Wide World 9, dated 1823. It begins with very traditional images as Emerson seeks the means of building a bridge to divinity:

> Human curiosity is forever engaged in seeking out ways & means of making a connection between the mind & the world of matter without or the world of mind that has subsisted here or an uniting bridge which shall join to future ages our own memory & deeds. This laudable curiosity should not neglect the formation of a bond which proposes to unite it not to men, to matter, or to beasts, but to the Unseen Spirit of the Universe. Our native delight in the intercourse of other beings urges us to cultivate with assiduity the friendship of great minds. But there is a Mind to whom all their greatness is vanity & nothing; who did himself create and communicate all the intellect that exists; & there is a mode of intercourse provided by which we can approach this excellent majesty. That Mind is God; and that Mode is Prayer.[4]

Prayer for the mature Emerson came to mean reflection, meditation on the nature, the presence and will of God, the search for God's law in the world. Prayer, as he put it, "does not at all consist in words but wholly is a state of mind."[5] In his view, "God enforces the law . . . to make the perfection of man's nature consist in a fixed equilibrium of the body & the mind."[6] Obedience to the law, then, results in an equilibrium in body and mind. Mastery of the law means a consistent equilibrium and an opportunity to know God's will.

During this period Emerson was still influenced by the rhetorical style and vision of his former teacher William Ellery Channing, in particular by a lecture delivered at Harvard in 1821, entitled "The Evidence of Revealed Religion." In the lecture, which Emerson greatly admired, Channing had said:

> The religion bears the mark of having come from a being who perfectly understood the human mind, and had power to provide for its progress. This feature of Christianity is of the nature of prophecy.[7]

Channing's willingness to move the traditional Christian message into the new realm of what we might call "mind studies" marks him as part of the new thinking at Harvard. The idea of "power to provide for its progress" opened the door to effective development of human understanding, rejecting the traditional view that revelation had ceased with the record only in sacred texts.

Later in 1823, in Wide World 10, Emerson develops this theme and attaches to it a natural appetite for such revelation from human nature.

> Mind, which is the end & aim of all Divine Operations, feeds with unsated appetite upon moral & material Nature, that is, upon the order of things which He has appointed. It is perpetually growing wiser & mightier by digesting this immortal food, and even in our feeble conceptions of the heavenly hosts we seek to fill up the painful chasm that divides God from his humble creatures upon earth by a magnificent series of godlike intellects. . . . But Man, in his nook of earth, knits his brow at the name of his Maker, & gravely apprehends that the discussion of his laws may lead to fanaticism.[8]

This early rhetoric, although heavily weighted with Calvinist images of feeble human beings knitting their collective brow as they lean over the chasm of ignorance, nonetheless reveals Emerson's early efforts at making a bridge of eloquence over that chasm. What, he wanted to know, is this passion to *know*, this "unsated appetite" to feed on things divine? It must be that the laws of the human mind have been formed with this overwhelming desire to know, just as Plato and Aristotle had stated. A bit further on, he reflects that "Mind . . . *expands* as it proceeds . . ."[9] a fact that suggests a universal plan in which human beings are crucial participants, not just individually but collectively.

Emerson's struggle to make a connection, to bridge the chasm of understanding, reaches an important stage in 1824, in Wide World 13. Here he realizes that all attempts at understanding must finally be fleshed out in language, specifically in metaphor, and that these images are the planks in the bridge—or, as he has it from the French preacher Jacques Saurin, "The world is the scaffold of Divine Justice."

> All Metaphysicians are mortified to find how entirely the whole materials of understanding are derived from sense. No man is understood who speculates on mind or character until he borrows the /emphatic/specific/ imagery of Sense . . . I fear the progress of Metaphysical philosophy may be found to consist in nothing else than the progressive introduction of apposite metaphors. Thus the Platonists congratulated themselves for ages upon their knowledge that the Mind was a dark chamber whereon ideas like shadows were painted. Men derided this as infantile when they afterwards learned that the Mind was a sheet of white paper whereon any & all characters might be written. Almost every thing in language that is bound up in your memory is of this significant sort.[10]

From the allegory of the cave from Plato's *Republic* (Book VII) to Locke's *tabula rasa* upon which experience writes its tales, human beings seize upon images, store them in memory, and then gradually form their own metaphysic. That Emerson, at this early stage in his career as writer and thinker, could see the mind's tendency intuitively to make metaphors from experience speaks to his growing understanding of the complexity of the laws of the mind. He was training his eye to observe the emerging metaphors and to test them against his growing understanding.

### ENTER SAMPSON REED

Fellow Bostonian Sampson Reed, three years Emerson's senior, had also gone to Harvard and the Divinity College. He had failed to complete his studies, however, and was by 1826 a pharmacist. In 1821, as a thesis for his Master's degree, Reed delivered an oration on genius that

Emerson greatly admired. In his journal for 1821, Emerson reflected on Reed's vision of the abyss of human existence:

> Mr S. Reed saith in Oration in 1821—"The people of the golden age have left us no monuments of genius, no splendid columns, no paintings, no poetry; they possessed nothing which evil passions might not obliterate, and when the heavens were rolled together as a scroll the curtain dropped between the world and their existence."
>
> Men live as if a curtain should be drawn between this scene of things & all after-existence. Perhaps they believe that they shall live again—but there is no recollection beyond the grave. In vain; there is a recollection—and an account; there are a thousand connecting cords stretching from this world to the next. Every action here of merit & of demerit, reaches out the dark valley to the centre of a mightier system with all its attendance of consequences & conditions infinitely various. Your actions have gone before you & united themselves with fearful alacrity to their final recompenses.[11]

Emerson's rhapsody on the afterlife and eternal justice emerges here from Reed's vision of oblivion, his glimpse into the dark chasm of human existence in time. Coming as it did from the other side of the mystical edge, Emerson's instinct always was to shed light into that chasm. His Platonic metaphor of a "thousand connecting cords stretching from this world to the next" affirms the immortality of human actions and their link to the "mightier system" beyond our knowledge and understanding.

Five years later, in 1926, Reed published his own declaration of faith, the hundred-page *Observations on the Growth of the Mind.* In his journal for September of that year, Emerson noted his admiration for Reed's work—even moved to call it "revelation," so much did it demonstrate to him both originality and truth. The impression on Emerson would not be merely momentary. Indeed, Emerson would incorporate many of Reed's *Observations* into his own *Nature* ten years later and even late in life would list Reed as "one of his men." In many ways

Reed was the John the Baptist of Transcendentalism and his *Observations* his call to "Make Way!"

Comparing these two works now, we become conscious of the attempt of both writers to bridge the abyss of the Unknown from different points on the metaphysical compass. Whereas Reed ventures out into the dark from the shores of human experience reflected in natural science combined with faith, Emerson projects his "thousand cords" and light from more ancient sources based in the creative imagination. And yet, Emerson's vision was more grounded in many respects, having its basis in consciousness.

In later years, Reed would have nothing good to say in behalf of the Transcendental movement. When the two disagreed over the philosophy of Swedenborg, for example, of whose thinking Reed was a major supporter as a member of the New Church, Reed told Emerson, "It is not so in your experience, but it is so in the other world." Emerson responded, "Other world? There is no other world; here or nowhere is the whole fact."[12]

In the light of our expanding imagery of the abyss, the chasm between the human and divine worlds, this comment by Emerson deserves closer inspection. As he matured, Emerson became convinced that to speak of "other worlds" was in error, was in fact what he would call "demonology." He saw in Swedenborg the limitations of a private metaphysical vision which was "other" in character. The world of angels and supernatural powers, Emerson believed, could give us no support or aid in any of our speculations or longings. Emerson's convictions centered instead on the concept of the cosmic One Mind, with that mind accessible to any and everyone, given the desire to know and the capacity to understand. To shoot the gulf, as it were, and lay claim to sights and sounds alien to human life "on the other side" was, at the very least, irrelevant, if not downright false.

Indeed, in a letter written to Carlyle in 1834, Emerson reflected on the import of Swedenborgism to his own perceptions of divinity:

It is only when they come to their descriptive theism, if I may say so, and then to their drollest heaven, and to some autocratic not moral decrees of God, that the mythus loses me.[13]

For Emerson, no theory of the Godhead smacking of the autocratic would ever coincide with his understanding of the divine/human interrelationship.

For the moment, however, in the 1820s Reed and Emerson were on the same path and shared the same vision. In his *Observations* Reed had made no reference to Swedenborg, staying with the more tangible arguments of natural science. In the interest of Mind and its capacity to reach out into nature to grasp its laws and to reach back within to discover its own, Reed's essay was crucial to Emerson's development as thinker, writer, and visionary. Reed opened his essay in a style and imagery unique to American writing to that time.

> . . . The mind has attained an upward and onward look, and is shaking off the errors and prejudices of the past. . . . The loud call on the past to instruct us, as it falls on the Rock of Ages, comes back in echo from the future. . . . We appear to be approaching an age which will be the silent pause of merely physical force before the powers of the mind; the timid, subdued, awed condition of the brute, gazing on the erect and godlike form of man.[14]

These images set the stage for the argument to follow. Emerson's intuitive sense of human possibility and his growing understanding of the ground on which his own being would set its foundation, heard in Reed's image of "the erect and godlike form of man" a call to rise up from the stooped posture of the fallen Adamic Man cast from Eden and instead to seek a transformation to what Emerson would later call full self-recovery. Emerson's own self-accusatory reflections of timidity in the face of an uncertain future, his own lack of vigor, combined with periods of ill health, all these facts of his own struggle found a willing listener for Reed's call to the erect position and a mind open to new hope and life-enhancing progress.

Here was a position in a middle ground between a sin-drenched, guilt-ridden humility and a self-proclaimed affirmative egotism. Reed did not proclaim victory in a world as one "insensible to its evils." Nor did his words emerge from a "feeling of self-admiration." Brilliantly, he placed the present human condition in religious perspective:

Since the fall of man, nothing has been more difficult for him than to know his real condition, since every departure from divine order is attended with a loss of the knowledge of what it is.

The question, then, for Reed was: "How can human beings determine their real condition?" So much mood and circumstance contrive to dictate our opinions of ourselves that our "real condition" is at best elusive.

Most of our knowledge implies relation and comparison. It is not difficult for one age, or one individual, to be compared with another; but this determines only their relative condition. The actual condition of man can be seen only from the relation in which he stands to his immediate Creator; and this relation is discovered from the light of revelation, so far as, by conforming to the precepts of revelation, it is permitted to exist according to the laws of divine order.

And, Reed's argument goes, the divine order is revealed in the laws of the mind. In fact, while human beings have been occupied with their own temporal affairs, "the sure but secret influence of revelation has been gradually changing the moral and intellectual character of the world." What Reed then does is to introduce a new philosophy based on the observation of the laws of mind.

The laws of the mind are in themselves fixed and perfect as the laws of matter; but they are laws from which we have wandered. There is a philosophy of the mind, founded not on the aspect it presents in any part or in any period of the world, but on its immutable relations to its first cause . . .

Reed develops this philosophy through an analysis of the nature of time, which, he observes, is a human invention and in its practical uses blinds us to the eternal nature of divine revelation. His equation, "Eternity is to the mind what time is to nature" illustrates the principle that our attempts to portray the Divine Nature with images of time and space—in other words, in terms of personified imagery—are destined to failure and delusion. As we shall see later, our images of a "personal God" are very much bound up in this perceptual problem, and numerous philosophical and religious arguments turn on this misunderstanding. The question, then, arises:

> What then is that development which the nature of the human mind requires? What is that education which has heaven for its object, and such a heaven as will be the effect of the orderly growth of the spiritual man?

Reed argues that just as the natural sciences are an outgrowth of the *structure* of the mind, philosophy is the outgrowth of the *purpose,* or *telos,* of the mind. By extension, the world, or nature, exists to "draw forth the latent energies of the soul." This energy is manifest in our innate love of nature and our gradual understanding of that love in relation to deeper values hidden beneath the surfaces of things. The sign we have of this understanding comes from the affection we feel in the presence of nature, human relations, and worship. Extending this affection into disciplined self-inquiry stimulates the growth of the mind to its proper dimensions.

This argument unites feeling, intellect, and devotion into a single vision of the growth of the mind. Emerson's instinctive desire to find the unities in things was strongly attracted to Reed's arguments here. The next step in the synthesis was to find a place for the imagination, that faculty of the mind abandoned by the Enlightenment in its rush to find a scientific basis for philosophic truth. As Reed points out, "the imagination was permitted for ages to involve the world in darkness, by putting theory in the face of fact." What was needed next was a renewal of the power of the imagination, the poetic spirit, to embrace the facts of existence within the embrace of the creative spirit of God.

> It belongs to the true poet to feel this spirit, and to be governed by it; to be raised above the senses; to live and breathe in the inward efforts of things; to feel the power of creation, even before he sees the effect; to witness the innocence and smiles of nature's infancy, not by extending the imagination back to chaos, but by raising the soul to nature's origin. The true poetic spirit, so far from misleading any, is the strongest bulwark against deception. It is the soul of science. Without it, the latter is a cheerless, heartless

study, distrusting even the presence and power of Him to whom it owes its existence.

The high chant of this passage inspired Emerson, whose own ambition was to elevate his thought to eloquence. It is this high chant to which Harold Bloom refers in *Agon* when he proclaims his own dogma for the American Religion: "It cannot become the American religion until it first is canonized as American literature."[15] Emerson's decision not to enter the marketplace as a philosopher *per se* but rather as an essayist and poet reflects his concern to re-invent Imagination as a faculty to uncover the truth of reality.

Central to that development is the recognition from each individual of that unique quality of mind that suggests a specific direction in life. Reed concludes *Observations* with an examination of that unique aspect of mind. His ideas are strongly echoed in Emerson's later work, particularly "Self-Reliance" and "Spiritual Laws," a further testament to the value of Reed's work in its own right.

> Every individual also possesses peculiar powers, which should be brought to bear on society in the duties best fitted to receive them. The highest degree of cultivation of which the mind is capable, consists in the most perfect development of that peculiar organization, which as really exists in infancy as in maturer years. . . . There is something which every one can do better than any one else; and it is in the tendency, and must be the end, of human events, to assign to each his true calling.

If we consider the following passage from "Spiritual Laws," so familiar to lovers of Emerson, we hear the clear echo of Reed. We also see how the powers of the poet, the ideal Reed held up as the great hope of the new philosophy, engage the thought and take it to new heights.

> Each man has his own vocation. The talent is the call. There is one direction in which all space is open to him. He has faculties silently inviting him thither to endless exertion. He is like a ship in a river; he runs against obstructions on every side but one; on that side all obstruction is taken away, and he sweeps serenely over a deepening channel into an infinite sea. This talent and this call

depend on his organization, or the mode in which the general soul incarnates itself in him. He inclines to do something which is easy to him, and good when it is done, but which no other man can do. He has no rival. For the more truly he consults his own powers, the more difference will his work exhibit from the work of any other. His ambition is exactly proportioned to his powers. . . . By doing his work, he makes the need felt which he can supply, and creates the taste by which he is enjoyed. By doing his own work, he unfolds himself.

What Emerson owes to Reed here is clear. What is also clear is the genius in Emerson's transformation of the ideas into poetic expression. The weakness of Reed's work, the reason that *Observations* is not part of the American canon, is that its second half reverts to sermonizing and holds too closely to traditional biblical authority. Reed's instincts were both radical and insightful, but his productivity has found no permanent recognition in the American Renaissance in which Emerson, Thoreau, and Whitman hold the honored places.

As 1826 came to a close and the new year began with illness and an uncertain future, Emerson reviewed the progress in his search for the laws of the mind and those cords which stretch to the infinite.

But the eye of the mind has at least grown richer in its hoard of observations. It has detected more of the darkling lines that connect past events to the present, and the present to the future; that run unheeded, uncommented in a thousand mazes wherever society subsists and are the moral cords of men by which the Deity is manifested to the vigilant or more truly to the illuminated observer . . . he has an instinctive dread of the tendencies to harmony in the Universe which he has often observed, & which betoken some future violence to root out this disorder. If the string cannot be made to accord, it must be broken.[16]

The young hero finds himself in the thousand mazes of his own mind, perceiving there discrepancies and dark contradictions. All he has is a golden cord that connects him to the light and to the harmony of the universe, from which discord of his mind may exclude him.

# *4*    EARLY VISIONS OF GOD

*In 1826* Emerson entered a personally turbulent ten-year span. He began to think more about the actual experience of human life, rather than studious preparation for it. The word "experience" has its roots in the Latin *experientia,* the "act of trying," meaning proof or trial. Experience in this sense is what became the center of Emerson's new life.

His reluctant decision to enter the ministry, which he did formally on October 10, 1826, resulted in an enviable appointment as Junior Minister at the Second Church in Boston, the church of the Mathers. Although he gave himself fully to these new responsibilities, his instincts, expressed both physically and emotionally, revealed the error he had made in the choice of a calling. Later, in the light of reflection, this experience would inform important insights into the nature of true calling in what he would call the escape from false ties.[1]

During this early period of his ministry, he fought poor health and dissatisfaction with his institutional accommodations by taking leave for a journey to St. Augustine, Florida. There, his consumptive lungs gradually healed and his low weight returned to normal. But his growing skepticism brought new strictures. One vivid example of the tensions working on him was noted in his journal for February 25, 1827:

> A fortnight since I attended a meeting of the Bible Society. The Treasurer of this institution is Marshall of the district & by a somewhat unfortunate arrangement had appointed a special meeting of the Society & a Slave Auction at the same hour & place, one being in the Government house & the other in the adjoining yard. One ear therefore heard the glad tidings of great joy whilst the other

was regaled with "Going gentlemen, Going! And almost without changing our position we might aid in sending scriptures into Africa or bid for "four children without the mother who had been kidnapped therefrom."2

That Emerson waited nearly two weeks before recording this experience is instructive. The account is rendered with sarcastic wit on both sides, from the "glad tidings of great joy" to the "Going gentlemen, Going!" We sense Emerson's disgust with both worlds. That he felt trapped in the need to accommodate his moral outrage to hypocrisies in both secular and religious worlds is evident. In the same entry Emerson notes that in listening to a local pastor "it really exceeded all power of face to be grave during the divine's very plain analysis . . . " This is more than mere Cambridge superiority. The profession itself is coming under attack.

What Emerson desperately needed at this time was a worthy conversationalist, one who could both challenge his emerging doubts and provide a foil to his intuitive convictions. In Charleston, South Carolina, while sailing north in the spring of 1827, he encountered such a foil in the person of Achille Murat, a wealthy young plantation owner and nephew to Napoleon. By his own testimony, Murat was an atheist; but because he was also cultured, curious, and well-educated, he was a delightfully challenging companion for the young Emerson for more than a week.

Just prior to their meeting, Emerson had noted in his journal: "To believe too much is dangerous because it is near neighbor of unbelief. Pantheism leads to Atheism."3 Murat stood nearly in the same place as Emerson, that is, combining a great love of truth with a willingness to look at all sides of a question. As Emerson described the encounter:

> A new event is added to the quiet history of my life. I have connected myself by friendship to a man who with as ardent a love of truth as that which animates me, with a mind surpassing mine in the variety of its research, & sharpened & strengthened to an energy for *action*, to which I have no pretension by advantages of birth & practical connexion with mankind beyond almost all men in the world . . .4

The admiration for Murat expressed here borders on envy. Emerson, the poor cleric, confined by illness and circumstances to a relative passivity, saw in Murat what he would later say in *Representative Men* about his uncle as the admirable man of action. After their conversations, however, Emerson could say with conviction that although Murat was an atheist, his own faith was strongly held. Murat was

> . . . a consistent Atheist, and a disbeliever in the existence, &, of course, in the immortality of the soul. My faith in these points is strong & I trust, as I live, indestructible. Meantime I love & honour this intrepid doubter. His soul is noble, & his virtue as the virtue of a Sadducee must always be, is sublime.[5]

The conversations with Murat were crucial. For Emerson, coming north from the swamps of mindless faith where no one could engage him in any sort of intelligent discussion, Murat was a blessing. Here was a man who could penetrate beyond the sectarian illusions of institutionalized religion and, framing his views with a sophisticated Continental rhetoric, engage Emerson where it mattered. Emerson, on the other hand, respected Murat's arguments, and the two must have moved around the topic with much mutual admiration. A second journal reference to Murat as a man of the world makes the point.

> Yet my friend is at home in both these jarring empires and whilst he taxes my powers in his philosophic speculations can excel the coxcombs, & that, *con amore*, in the fluency of nonsense. Nevertheless I cannot but remember that God is in the heavens, God is here, and the eye of my friend is dull & blind and cannot perceive Him.[6]

The theme of the opaque and transparent eye would return often in Emerson's judgments. Later in the same journal Emerson wrote Murat's name at the heading of a long Latin passage copied out carefully from Francis Bacon's complete works, the passage having to do with "Poesy" or the powers of the Imagination as a faculty of the mind. Emerson must have perceived in the passage an argument to counter Murat's opacity. The relevant part of the passage is its second half:

> And therefore, since the acts and events which are the subjects of

real history are not of sufficient grandeur to satisfy the human mind, Poesy is at hand to feign acts more heroical; since the successes and issues of actions as related in true history are far from being agreeable to the merits of virtue and vice, Poesy corrects it, exhibiting events and fortunes as according to merit and the law of providence; since true history wearies the mind with satiety or ordinary events, one like another, Poesy refreshes it, by reciting things unexpected and various and full of vicissitudes. So that this Poesy conduces not only to delight but also to magnanimity and morality.[7]

Imagination, inspired as revelation by God, enters the mind to act not only as leaven to ordinary existence but also as mediator to a higher level of perception. For Emerson at this point, the human mind, with its full range of faculties engaged, was the source of truth. Only the mind with a capacity for open reception, including the influence of Imagination, could approach the goals of both magnanimity and morality. Emerson's recent conversations with Murat were certainly magnanimous, or great-souled, in their openness. What Emerson took from them would serve him throughout his life, especially when less than magnanimous souls reacted to his own search for the truth.

## THE NATURE OF GOD

Emerson next re-entered his life as a minister and soon became a new husband, marrying the beautiful but frail Ellen Tucker of New Hampshire. He would encounter as never before the question of the presence of God in his life. Who and what is God? Does God interact with the creation, with human life? If yes, how? What images or metaphors can express this identity and this interaction? These are the questions that occupied Emerson throughout the next several years in the science of God-knowing—which he called Theoptics, or Visions of God.[8]

If Emerson's fundamental contributions to theological speculations were merely to assert that "God is within" or that human beings perfect themselves by imagining a perfect deity toward which they strive to perfect themselves, we would not be much interested in his thought. These ideas, if not considered totally orthodox by Christian standards, are nonetheless ordinary by thoughtful theological standards. We are looking for more. By more, we mean not only answers to questions about the nature of God as creator of the cosmos and what we might mean by a "personal" God, but also in what ways Emerson's lifelong inquiry informs the major themes of religion in America. By all accounts a vast majority of Americans believe in God, or at least say they do when asked. And yet, for many who no longer attend church or have a religious affiliation, such belief may well be superficial, based primarily on simplistic notions or habitual thinking from a traditional past. Emerson's thoughtful pursuit of the nature of the Infinite serves as a rational guide to discovering a more coherent and personal vision, one that informs intellectual understanding as well as the conduct of life.

We begin our examination of Emerson's visions of God with the commencement of his formal duties as a Unitarian minister at Second Church in Boston and his marriage to Ellen Tucker, both of which took place in 1829. Both events relate to his intellectual inquiries at this time: In the first instance, he was a hesitant pastor searching for a true path within the Church; in the second, he was a warm, attentive husband deeply in love. The combination sent him searching for God with both mind and heart wide open and receptive to each new experience.

He noted at this time, "Immense significance to the precept *Know Thyself.*"[9] This inwardness has special significance now that he had, as it were, begun to live. He was no longer the passive consumptive lolling away the hours in Florida sunshine, existing as a kind of contemplative fever in matter, to paraphrase Thomas Mann's definition of life. His new responsibilities kept his schedule full; and although Ellen's health was poor and even declining in this period, he remained hopeful for their future. He had recovered, after all. So might she. He also pushed at the limits of traditional sermonizing, venturing into territory uncommon to the pulpits of the time.

We cannot help but wonder how the parishioners of the Second Church responded to the sermon (#LXVI) he delivered on February 14, 1830. It contained much of the following from his journal for February 11:

Every man makes his own religion, his own God, his own charity; takes none of these from the Bible or his neighbor, entire. All feel that there is something demanded by the mind stronger & wiser than itself. . . . it would seem this idea is pointed at in all the structure of the animal, man. As nothing . . . is made without a meaning . . . is this *leaning* without a purpose disclosed as we study it, well then, is this *leaning* without a purpose . . . is it not a finger pointing straight upwards at the Great Spirit? Then it is found that this superstition is cleansed into religion as the mind is formed.[10]

Emerson is willing and determined to attack the question of the nature of God from perspective of the developing mind. He remains on the human side of the chasm, feeling, perhaps, that most people have a whole series of images grafted to their consciousness from the Bible, from Sunday School, and from cultural mythology. The need as he saw it was for balance, to redirect the point of inquiry to the individual mind and to see religion for what it is. Indeed, the day before (February 10) he had written to himself that

The character of each man shall form his Imagination. The Beings of the imagination shall become objects of unshaken faith, that is, to his mind, Realities. As the man becomes wiser these subjective deities & demons approximate those of the good mind—that is, truth . . .[11]

This firm connection, creating an identity, between the truth and the "good mind" gives us an indication of where Emerson's inquiries are headed. He will not be satisfied with a subjective image of God created by an individual mind. In other words, he will not leave us with a completely relativistic view in which we are all free to imagine whatever deity pleases us. The good mind comes near to the truth insofar as we approach whatever state that might be. Knowing in what "the good mind" consists grafts Platonic thought onto the search.

In this progression Emerson does not parallel Voltaire's dictum, "If God did not exist, it would be necessary to invent Him." On the contrary he maintains a fundamental faith in the actual existence (in some form) of deity, which human beings approach by virtue of Imagination and truth-seeking working together. To this point then, Emerson's conclusion is that God is "the most elevated conception of character that can be formed in the mind."[12] But it is also, at the same time, "the individual's own soul carried out to perfection."

These passages reflect the intellect at work, the most that the understanding can say about the unknown. Emerson has no interest in logical attacks up the summit of deity. His instincts will take him into a gnostic poesy and to the conclusion that spiritual facts are their own evidence. We have to approach matters of Spirit spiritually, and Emerson's "good mind" is primarily a spiritual, moral mind; it looks at the world and at daily life as spiritual in nature. To see spiritually is to know spirit. Life's experiences, therefore, are essentially spiritual in nature and import.

Meanwhile, experience was also cruel. Almost a year to the day of these entries in his journal, Emerson made the following brief note:

Ellen Tucker Emerson died 8th February. Tuesday morning 9 o'clock.[13]

Ellen's death was not unexpected, given her history of lung problems and her own fatalistic pronouncements. She seemed to know that she and Waldo would not grow old together, and that she would not bear him children. Nonetheless, to lose her love and company after barely seventeen months of marriage was devastating. To this point in his life, at age twenty-eight, Emerson also had lost his father and a sister, both before he was twelve. After Ellen, he would lose his two brothers to tuberculosis as well, and his son Waldo Jr., age five, all in a decade. In terms of intimacy and intense feelings of love, the loss of Ellen would be the most difficult to bear.

In the next few months his journal entries were unusual for their personal nature. Nearly a week after her death, on February 13, Emerson made the following entries, here somewhat edited to highlight images of God and traditional religious imagery:

Five days are wasted since Ellen went to heaven to see, to know, to worship, to love, to intercede. God be merciful to me a sinner & repair this miserable debility in which her death has left my soul.

. . . Pray for me Ellen & raise the friend you so truly loved, to be what you thought him. . . . Dear Ellen (for that is your name in heaven) shall we not be united even now more & more, as I more steadfastly persist in the love of truth & virtue which you loved? Spirits are not deceived & now you know the sins & selfishness which the husband would fain have concealed from the confiding wife—help me to be rid of them. . . . Reunite us, o thou Father of our Spirits.[14]

These images of God, heaven, spirits, and the nature of the afterlife evoke all the traditional images of a personal God, a heavenly rest for sainted persons, and life everlasting for the human personality, at least in some form retaining identity. These and passages like them have prompted critics to accuse Emerson of theological inconsistencies, especially comparing these images to pronouncements in the essays over the next ten years.

Other interpretations, however, are possible. First, when grief overwhelms the intellect and feeling rises up to claim center stage, the images of a caring, personal God, a heaven for departed souls, and an immortality of the individual psyche ease the pain. This interpretation, certainly offered before, tends to excuse Emerson, as something like an admission of weakness. Another interpretation, however, is more consistent with his faith and fundamental intellectual honesty.

Emerson regarded matters of divine revelation and the existence of God as a two-sided coin. On his own side, where the mind receives metaphoric data from beyond the chasm of the unknown, Emerson continually pursued knowledge of God and the infinite according to intuition, reason, and experience. On the other side of the coin, or chasm, however, lies what human beings can never truly know. In this realm, which can only be expressed in the language of faith, is situated the faith of the fathers and the imagery of tradition. In his grief, then, Emerson called upon this tradition, not to contradict his own understanding, but to express, in crisis, his abiding faith.

At this point in his life, as a minister, a widower, a young man with uncertain views, this faith in the traditional tropes of Christianity stood against despair. In this light, for example, it is not contradictory for

Emerson to record ten days later, on February 23, the following observation on the words of the great Neoplatonist Plotinus:

> It is worth recording that Plotinus said, "Of the Unity of God,
> Nothing can be predicated, neither being, nor essence, nor life, for
> it is above all these." Grand it is to recognize the truth of this & of
> every one of that first class of truths which are *necessary* [empha-
> sis Emerson's] . . .[15]

Then he quotes a series of what he termed "quasi truths."

> "God without can only be known by God within," & "the Scrip-
> tures can be explained only by that Spirit which dictated them."
> . . . It would be well for every mind to collect with care every truth
> of this kind he may meet, & make a catalogue of "necessary truths."
> They are scanned & approved by the Reason far above the under-
> standing. They are the last facts by which we approximate
> metaphysically to God.[16]

This sequence illustrates the dual nature of Emerson's perceptions
at this time and the shifts he made in locating the sources of his faith.
References to "Reason" (here capitalized) and "understanding" in the
passage above come from Emerson's reading of Coleridge, whose distinctions are that Reason is that part of the mind capable of receiving
divine truths and understanding is a lower, strictly human faculty.

Reason is the faculty that allows Emerson to make the following
observations in his journal exactly one month later, on March 13, 1831:

> Every word of truth that is spoken by man's lips is from God. Every
> thought that is true is from God. Every right act is from God . . .
> I suppose that miraculous power is only more power, not differ-
> ent power. I suppose it is strictly of the same kind, for I suppose
> there is but one kind. There is one source of power [—] that
> is God.[17]

Emerson's interesting phrase "I suppose" reveals the way his mind
approaches these assertions. "I suppose" can mean "it seems" as much
as it means "I conclude."

This entry comes under the heading in Emerson's journals of

"Theoptics," which the editors of the journals suggest may mean "a transcendental perspective of time and of the single soul infused into all phenomena."[18] Such an idea is reflected in November of 1831 as Emerson tells himself to be patient in his dealings with the religiously orthodox as he copes with the challenges of being their pastor:

> You can't be true to their principles but you can to yours now in sitting with them. Your understanding of religion is that it is doing right from a right motive. Stick to that mighty sense. Don't affect the use of an adverb or an epithet more than belongs to the feeling you have. . . . As religious philosophy advances, men will cease to say 'the future state' & will say instead 'the whole being.'[19]

As he grows in understanding, Emerson warns himself to remain true to the moral foundation of religion even as he develops his philosophical understanding of its sources and nature. The idea of "whole being" is another suggestion of his concept of One World in which human beings, God, and Great Unity all reside together. The chasm of understanding, then, which the mind cannot bridge alone, is nonetheless a part of this "whole being." Finding the right word for this wholeness and being will be the challenge of the future, finding the right adverb and epithet as occasion demands, but, as he warns himself, not in sentimentality, or in excess of feeling.

## CRISIS OF PROFESSION

By the summer of 1832, during a cold June in Boston, the crisis over his profession gathered heat in Emerson's mind. His thoughts were turning more and more to leaving the Church.

> I have sometimes thought that in order to be a good minister it was necessary to leave the ministry. The profession is antiquated. In an altered age, we worship in the dead forms of our forefathers. Were not a Socratic paganism better than an effete superannuated Christianity?[20]

He took a leave again from his duties and went to Conway, New Hampshire, to reflect. In the mountains, where a human being could move within a more vertical landscape, Emerson reflected that he ought to see, from such heights and depths, his human situation more clearly. Nature was teaching him. Speaking of the divine principle, he said:

> We know little of its laws—but we have observed that a north wind clear cold with its scattered fleet of drifting clouds braced the body & seemed to reflect a similar abyss of spiritual heaven between clouds in our minds . . .[21]

We know as much as we can clearly observe around us. Everything speaks to us, and the world in its forms, its hours creeping or flying by, its clouds and darkness, its people and creatures, all instruct, suggest, and lead. If the world is an image of the divine principle, then this spiritual world reflects its laws, which in turn can be followed, teaching us our duties and directing our will.

The summer mountains of New Hampshire led Emerson to his decision to resign as Junior Minister of the Second Church. Although the issue that served as the point of contention was the ritual of Communion, The Lord's Supper, Emerson really took his leave for the larger reason of his intellectual convictions. Stronger than his sense of duty and the long tradition of the Emersons in the Church was his personal rebellion from the dying rituals of Christian worship. At heart he was a rebel with a radical agenda. The only real question was "How shall I live? What shall be my outward calling?"

# 5                          THE CALLING

*Emerson's European* journey, which lasted eight months during 1833, was modeled after the classic "grand tour." It was notable in its first half, the Italian tour, for his growing appreciation of liturgical and classical art. He paid his respects to all the great figures of the Italian Renaissance and the Greek and Roman past. In the Church of San Croce in Florence, for example, his "flesh crept" as he stood over the dust of Michelangelo, and he visited the Pitti Palace twice to see the famous Venus de' Medici, walking around and around it, marveling at its beauty.

Like all tourists in foreign lands, Emerson felt the sense of separation caused by language barriers and the confinements of spending hours in close contact with unchosen traveling companions. On frequent walks alone, his solitary temperament attracted him to monasteries. On the island of Sicily, at Syracuse, he visited the Latomie of the Gardens of the Capuchins, where he was, by his own testimony, seriously tempted to remain for several weeks. In his journal for February 25, he wrote, "How good & pleasant to stop & recollect myself in this worn out nook of the human race, to turn over its history & my own."[1]

This tendency toward private reflection had been a part of Emerson's life for a long time. His was not the practice of meditation in the Oriental pattern of sitting in a particular posture for a set amount of time and emptying the mind of conscious thought. Rather, Emerson sat in silence, allowing thoughts to arise, or bubble up, in mind where he reflected upon them, writing down clarified observations when moved to do so. His writing style, so troubling to some critics looking for more developed strains of sequential argument, emerged from this reflective discipline. He cultivated a lifelong habit of culling passages from the deposits of such observations he had made in his "savings bank," the term he used for his journals after 1833. When he did search his journals for apt passages, the test was the immediacy of the prose, some evidence of taking accurate dictation from his Muse. Anything "off line" he rejected.

The "act of reflection," as he called it at the beginning of "Spiritual Laws," allowed him to intuit the "still small voice" to which he wished to be obedient. If the messages he received from the depths of these reflections did not cohere as argument, he was not concerned. His interest was revelation, not argument, and he was aware that his habits of refection and his style of expressing its results might appear, to some, out of joint. On the boat back to America, he noted, "In this world, if a man sits down to think, he is immediately asked if he has the headache."[2]

The journey to Europe had taught Emerson the great lesson of self-reliance in matters of knowledge. He had gone to seek a teacher but had found nothing but dusty portraits and ordinary human beings like himself. His visits with the "great voices" of Europe such as Walter Landor, Coleridge, and Wordsworth proved unsatisfactory. These public figures were full of attitudes and opinions and lived within the aura of reputations earned long ago. Only Thomas Carlyle had proved an open, spirited man of genius, and the two spent a welcome two days of high discourse.

So it was that as he happily turned toward home, Emerson began to reflect on his future. His first book, *Nature,* was taking form in his notes and in his mind, and he began to think about how and where he would live. He knew he would not be a pastor again, but he was, after all, still ordained and could fill pulpits all over New England. Occasional Sundays, though, do not make a career. He would have loved to have survived as a poet, but he knew that was unlikely. Making a living as a writer of prose was also not feasible. So, what to do? The law had no appeal, nor did teaching. Ideas of a secular pulpit began to form.

As he left England, he was more certain about the course his life would take. What was uncertain was how he would support himself outside the Church.

> Back again to myself. I believe that the error of the religionists lies in this, that they do not know the extent or the harmony or the depth of their moral nature, that they are clinging to little, positive, verbal, formal versions of the moral law & very imperfect versions too, while the infinite laws, the laws of the Law, the great circling truths whose only adequate symbol is the material laws, the astronomy, &c, are all unobserved, & sneered at when spoken of, as frigid & insufficient.[3]

The triangulated references to extent, harmony, and depth would return again and again for Emerson. In particular, the idea or sense that *harmony* is a valuable and necessary symbol of the divine nature is thematic throughout. Harmony or concord implied not only peace and accord, but also lawfulness, from which he would later develop his laws of compensation and fate. From these attributes he was in a position to make as clear a statement as had ever come from his pen about the vision he was to articulate, whatever his means of earning a living would turn out to be.

> Let me enumerate a few of the remarkable properties of that [fundamental human] nature. A man contains all that is needful to his government within himself. He is made a law unto himself. All real good or evil that can befal him must be from himself. He only can do himself any good or any harm. Nothing can be given to him or taken from him but always there is a compensation. There is a correspondence between the human soul & everything that exists in the world. . . . The purpose of life seems to be to acquaint a man with himself. He is not to live to the future as described to him but to live to the real future by living to the real present. The highest revelation is that God is in every man.[4]

Keeping his attention on what he called "the real present" led him to several important life decisions. His first was to settle not in Boston but in Concord, the harmonious and pastoral home of his ancestors. The decision to live in this small country town was a victory of the rural existence over the urban. Boston was too distracting and would not give him time and quiet for reflection. Boston, like New York, had its own vibrant energies which were, for someone with his sensitivities, too imposing.

As to his future profession, a new cultural phenomenon met him when he returned from Europe: the opening up of the lyceum lecture circuit. These were gatherings, usually mid-week, of interested people to hear professional lecturers give talks on science, art, history, and culture. Emerson's decision to join the growing ranks of these speakers was a natural one. Each talk would last about fifty minutes, they could be formally prepared, and, most important, what he said would not have to conform to any institutional dogma or expectation.

Ostensibly he would remain away from religion and religious subjects in these lectures, concentrating instead on topics such as his first series on Natural History. But in fact he continued to supply pulpits around New England, having still a desire to articulate his sense of the laws of the Law. His journals for this period are full of observations about the human relationship to God. Throughout this period the journals are more interesting than the sermons and formal lectures as Emerson slowly, surely developed his more radical views.

As an indication of this developing aversive spirit, we often find Emerson reacting to his regular stops in other pastors' churches to listen to the Christian message. Typical was a visit to the Reverend Joseph Grafton's parish in Newtown on August 10, 1834. Emerson expressed his wonder that "such fatuity as Calvinism is now, should be able to stand yet . . . in the face of day." He then went on to state his own case in eloquent terms that would be reflected four years later in the "Address."

> Is it not time to present this matter of Christianity exactly as it is,
> to take away all the false reverence for Jesus, & not mistake the
> stream for the source? . . . God is in every man. God is in Jesus
> but let us not magnify any of the vehicles as we magnify the Infi-
> nite Law itself. We have defrauded him of his claim of love on all
> noble hearts by our superstitious mouth honour. We love Socrates
> but give Jesus the Unitarian Association.[5]

The attributes of human beings, especially if divinity dwells within

*Emerson home, "Bush," in Concord. Maintained as historical site.*

that fundamental nature, must in some measure reflect the attributes of God. Emerson asks, "Is not man in our day described by the very attributes which once he gave his God?"[6] Isn't our tendency to attribute to human beings the genius that produces invention and discovery? Isn't our "control" over the environment the role we once attributed to the minute handling of divinity?

What had happened was that the forms of religious expression had not kept pace with scientific discovery and revolutions in human knowledge. As Emerson toured the great European capitals, he witnessed centuries-old rituals encrusted with irrelevance. The churches were gathering dust, and the music and lifeless language rang hollow through cold, damp walls.

Why, he wondered, do we attend services at all? What is being served by these weekly excursions? Are they not an admission of our loss, our separation not only from God but from our own nature? Emerson would assert in the coming years that the proper search is for the essential unity inherent in the human and divine conditions. Our true celebration should be in likeness and not in difference, and certainly not in depravity. In these terms he spoke of the ideal of worship:

The very fact of worship declares that god is not at one with himself, that there are two gods. Now does this sound like high treason & go to lay flat all religion? It does threaten our forms but does not that very word "form" already sound hollow?[7]

The radical direction of this line takes us to what Joel Porte has called the unchurching of the New England mind,[8]—at least in the abolition of formal worship, although perhaps not the fellowship of like-minded people coming together to celebrate the presence of God in their lives, or the times in life when community gathers to hold up the fallen and the desolate.

What forms, then, will serve to awaken the perception of God within, of the presence of a divinity at the core of being? Emerson next makes a distinction between the *concept* of religion, as the quest for the values of an ideal life, versus the systems arrived at for the articulation of those values.

It threatens our forms but it does not touch injuriously Religion. Would there be danger if there were real religion? If the doctrine that God is in man were faithfully taught & received, if I lived to speak the truth & enact it, if I pursued every generous sentiment as one enamored, if the majesty of goodness were reverenced: would not such a principle serve me by way of police at least as well as a Connecticut Sunday?[9]

Emerson eventually answered his own question with the great law of Compensation, that understanding of how Providence balances every act with justice, punishes sin in the moment it is committed, and judges us with each word we utter. Emerson's concept of Compensation is the central figure of his portrait of human character. His essay of that title is similarly central to an understanding of the Essays, First Series.

Its crucial image is that "the dice of God are always loaded." The laws of the Law always demonstrate that fundamental precept: that God's law loads Plato's Good into the movement of the cosmos, and that all natural actions tend toward that ideal. We are in God's will insofar as we also move in that direction, consciously or not. The test, then, of our being coincident with the will of God is the extent to which our actions can be determined to be good actions. Against the claims of being simplistic, Emerson phrases the application of this law in human life:

> But the people, the people. You hold up your pasteboard religion for the people who are unfit for the true. So you say. But presently there will arise a race of preachers who will take such hold of the omnipotence of truth that they will blow the old falsehood to shreds with the breath of their mouth. There is no material show so splendid, no poem so musical as the great law of Compensation in our moral nature. When an ardent mind once gets a glimpse of that perfect beauty & sees how it envelopes him & determines all his being, will he easily slide back to a periodic shouting about "atoning blood?" I apprehend that the religious history of society is to show a pretty rapid abandonment of forms of worship & the renovation & exaltation of preaching into real anxious instruction.[10]

The word "anxious" here is used in its sense of avid and eager, rather than distressed, nervous, or the German *angst*. Also implied in the word is immediacy, the idea that real religious instruction examines us NOW, hence its anxiety. Emerson foresaw a time, only somewhat evident in our own day, when the great law of compensation would give human beings the ability to gauge in every action and thought the coincidence of that thought or action with the Law. The examined life is the means by which we determine that coincidence.

We may think in terms of conscience as the modifying power within us that warns us when we are about to act wrongly. Emerson's idea is different, however. According to his analysis of our moral nature, in which God resides as a living force, we are guided along the path of God's will as we listen and obey all in one motion. These principles are the true guide to all the virtues we hold dear.

> Democracy/Freedom has its root in the Sacred truth that every man hath in him the divine Reason [Law] or that though few men since the creation of the world live according to the dictates of Reason, yet all men are created capable of so doing. That is the equality & the only equality of all men. To this truth we look when we say, "Reverence thyself. Be true to thy self." Because every man has

within him somewhat really divine therefore is slavery the unpardonable outrage it is.[11]

These words were written only twelve years after the death of Thomas Jefferson, who when he died on July 4, 1826, still owned 130 slaves. Jefferson's call for fundamental equality as the basis of a democratic society, failed the test of personal action in the hypocrisy of his ownership of fellow human beings. His was a hypocrisy having its basis in a shallow understanding and not in personal, historical circumstances. If Jefferson had lived according to Emerson's law of compensation, either he would have sold his slaves or he would have never spoken of freedom and equality as a fundamental value to be cherished by freedom-loving human beings. To suggest, as many do, that Jefferson was justified by virtue of living in the midst of an established institution simply explains his actions, or lack of them; it does not minimize the contradiction.

The truth is that Jefferson's view of human beings in the racial sense was ruled by his deep prejudice against peoples of African origin, whom he held to be fundamentally inferior to people of European descent. His racial views overriding those of human nature in the abstract made his hypocrisy possible. In Emerson's case, the depth of his views moved beyond color to the core of human identity, and he returned from that providential territory with a higher knowledge. There can be no present or future dialogue between the races without that fundamental understanding. The differences between Jefferson and Emerson on this score make it evident that Emerson's vision is closer to the core of a genuine ideal of equality in America.

## THE OUTER CALLING

It was an easy step from the articulated certainty of Emerson's inner calling to the application of that calling to the world at large. As he filled pulpits throughout New England over the next few years, he also made himself available to the lyceum circuit. To the best of his ability, he merged his sermonizing, his lecturing, and his writing into a unified expression of his being. As we shall also see, this unity would also emerge in the fusion of thinking and writing, which would become the key to his genius. This wholeness or harmony of life gradually finds expression in the journals of late 1834 and the next several years.

For Emerson, compensation also meant that in the harmony of one's life, there are fit duties and apt opportunities for the natural and proper expression of calling: What a person can do, he or she will do and will have the chance to do. If today's parents and educators saw their task as awakening in the young their proper calling, we would have much greater harmony not only in the economy but also in the culture. Emerson's view began in the application of God-given talent.

> The blessed God has given to each his calling in his ruling love. Release by an act of law all men today from their contracts & all apprentices from their indentures & and pay all labor with equal wages & tomorrow you should find the same contracts redrawn[,] for one would choose to work in wood, another in stone, and a third in iron; one would prefer a farm, another the sea; one would paint, another sing; another survey land, another deal in horses; & another project adventures. God has adapted the brain & the body of men to the work that is to be done in the world.[12]

The tendency in our culture today is for "calling" to be driven by the marketplace, rather than by talent seeking its own proper expression. But it is wiser to watch the growing child for signs of talent and desire emerging from within, rather than from the media or parental projection. Nurturing individual calling into fruition is truly an expression of genius, which in turn is the sign of natural law in operation, because it finds its truth in the harmony of child and world. Emerson saw already in his own time the tendency—now standard in our "national" system of schooling—to impose learning (tuition) instead of drawing out each child's God-given abilities (intuition).

When Emerson looked objectively at his own talents, gradually nurtured them himself, and then stopped listening to various members of his family as they pushed him into the ministry, he was able to make the God-given choice. He was to be a lecturer/writer. He was to transform his insights and contemplations into images, which in turn he would set down in their natural order. He would, in fact, become an aphorism, a set of principles. As Coleridge would say, the best of men are an aphorism, and Emerson would follow this principle of personal development into fruition. The lyceum circuit beckoned, and he answered. With a wonderful touch of self-deprecating humor in December, 1834, exactly a year after his return from Europe, he sealed his choice for the future:

> Do, dear, when you come to write Lyceum lectures, remember that you are not to say, What must be said in a lyceum? but what discoveries or stimulating thoughts have I to impart to a thousand persons? not what they will expect to hear but what is fit for me to say.[13]

His emphasis upon "discoveries or stimulating thoughts" is an indication of the method of his inquiries. Emerson was a seeker in a territory he marked off as a new thing in nature. He would not follow anyone else's path, but rather report what progress he had made in the wilderness of his choosing. Marching off into the abyss to seek a proper "fit" there, he intended to report back what he discovered in its extremities. If the visions, in the form of metaphoric approximations, proved worthy, they could be measured by a fundamental standard, which Emerson expressed in his journal on Christmas Eve, 1834.

> Him I call rich, that soul I call endowed whether in man or woman, who by poverty or affliction or love has been driven home so far as to make acquaintance with the spiritual dominion of every human mind.[14]

As a writer, Emerson's most outstanding quality of mind was his power of discrimination. That quality, which we can further define as a discerning judgment separating fact from opinion—as opposed to a mere refined taste—allowed him to insert the sharpened blade of his insight between the layers of human experience, to peel away illusions, one by one, revealing the core, or pith of experience. As such we are dependent still upon that power and only need to learn how to read him well. Close reading develops our own powers of discrimination, which in turn we may apply to our own experience. In that sense Emerson is an exercise in discriminating reading as much as he is a seer of the truth.

# 6    SCYLLA AND CHARYBDIS

*On his* European sojourn Emerson had taken a steamboat from Messina en route to Naples and passed through the strait of Scylla and Charybdis. He noted in his journal that the great rock and whirling tides "have long lost their terrors . . . "[1] Now that he was back in Concord making his way in the world, these two mythical monsters loomed before him.

Confronting him was the task of presenting an exalted vision of human nature. On one hand, it had to be steered clear of the sin-drenched, Calvinist rock of Scylla. On the other hand, it had to evoke a vision of an immanent God who was in-dwelling, yet did not suggest the pantheistic oblivion of which Charybdis was an apt symbol. The term "pantheist" had been used by John Toland in 1705 with reference to Socinianism, the movement referred to by the Princeton trio in response to Emerson's Divinity College Address. In this usage, the idea that everything is God creates a false identity in which all resemblance vanishes, creating a false unity.

As Emerson began his own journey of discovery, he made note of the state of mind necessary to his task.

> The truest state of mind, rested in, becomes false. Thought is the manna which cannot be stored. It will be sour if kept, & tomorrow must be gathered anew. Perpetually must we East ourselves, or we get into irrecoverable error, starting from the plainest truth & keeping as we think the straightest road of logic. It is by magnifying God, that men become Pantheists; it is by piously personifying him, that they become idolaters.[2]

By "East ourselves," Emerson refers to finding the sun of truth each day, each moment. It was a phrase he adapted from Coleridge, "to find out the east for ourselves." He meant that we need the illuminating sunlight as we tend to deceive ourselves as we settle into the darkness of our beliefs, content with our certainties, only to discover one day that "we have had no sane moment."[3]

Because the Christian Church had placed Jesus Christ in a central position between God and humanity, making God transcendent and diminishing human beings, Emerson was forced to form a bridge between God and humanity through mind. By exploring both mind and nature, he hoped to bridge the chasm that had been created by removing Jesus from idolatry.

His beginning came with a strong statement of self-trust, one that would appear later in "Self-Reliance." A journal entry in June, 1835, contains this affirmation:

> Away with this succumbing & servility forever. I will not be warned of the sacredness of traditions. I will live wholly from within. You say they may be impulses from below[,] not from above. Maybe so. But if I am the Devil's child I will live from the Devil. I can have no sacred law but that of my nature.[4]

To form a bridge across the chasm of infinitude, Emerson had to build a strong foundation within his own nature. Not to do so would mean necessarily that doubt would cancel all his authentic impressions. He had faith that God would reveal the true nature of divinity on one side of this chasm. His task was to trust that his own mind was capable of receiving accurate nuances from the Great Silence. Discrimination was the proper measure and necessary faculty.

He called his task the First Philosophy, a term from Bacon's *Advancement of Learning*. Wondering who in Concord and beyond would ever be interested in his ruminations, he realized that perhaps no one would. By writing he could perhaps reach those souls capable of understanding his vision, but in ordinary rural activity he occasionally found himself alone with his thoughts among those more interested in the daily round. He also realized that the task of writing would not reveal the truth—no one could do that—but rather could only direct attention to where truth resides. He saw himself finding approaches, making refinements, and developing what he called a "proportioned strength of mind."[5]

The question became, then, "How is the mind strengthened?" Part of his process was to develop the practice of observing the mind at its work. Thus, in reflection it was not enough simply to look at the thoughts as they arose in mind; he had to look as well at the way the thoughts themselves come into being, in what shape they bubble to the surface or fly in the window. In other words, Emerson saw that thoughts arrive in images and that the translation of these images into prose or poems is a symbolic exercise.

> I believe I never take a step in thought when engaged in conversation without having some material symbol of my proposition figuring itself incipiently at the same time. My sentence often ends in babble from a vain effort to represent that picture in words. How much has a figure, an illustration availed every sect. As when the reabsorption of the soul into God was figured by a phial of water broken in the sea. . . . And I suppose that any man who will watch his intellectual process will find a material image cotemporaneous with every thought & furnishing the garment of the thought.[6]

It is indeed severe to say that we become the images we have of ourselves, and that we are shaped by self-images. By definition, an image is not identical to the thought it symbolizes; but an image either moves us or not according to how effectively it strikes home. Its aptness depends on how effectively it causes us to be struck by a blow of recognition *where we live*. Paying attention to these images and their effect is one of our measures of their "rightness" for a particular use.

Plato's allegory of the cave in the *Republic* is one powerful self-image. The description of being trapped, looking at the shadows of banal existence while the sunlight of spiritual truth burns outside, away from our knowledge and sight, both clarifies and creates a reality for human perception. Philosophy went to great lengths to deny the efficacy of that image when materialism took center stage in the drama of human history. Emerson's reference to the breaking of the phial in the great eternal sea is another compelling one, especially among those

whose image of the human soul corresponds to the image of water
being absorbed into the Great Soul of the universe upon the death of
the body.

As Emerson suggests, our images reveal something of our belief systems. Whether we see ourselves as breaking free of the illusions of the
cave to struggle upwards to the light, or as the blank slates of Locke's
*tabula rasa* upon which experience writes its story, or as intelligent apes
rising up from the ooze of time toward some accidental fate—whatever our choice of images—the important fact remains that images they
are, and that what reality they may or may not symbolize is the essential mystery to be penetrated.

Such are the attractions of image-making that we are captivated to
our possible detriment by its powers. Emerson reflected on that power
in his journal.

> We have little control of our thoughts. We are pensioners upon
> Ideas. They catch us up for brief moments into their heavens & so
> fully possess us that we take no thought for the morrow, gaze like
> children without an effort to make them our own. By & by we fall
> out of that rapture & then bethink us where we have been & what
> we have seen & go painfully gleaning up the grains that have fall-
> en from the sheaf.[7]

His mixing of metaphors in that description makes its own point
and is typical of his method of penetrating our awareness. As we see
the images, we are drawn into their influence, as pensioners, worshippers, children, and gleaners of the fields. So fleeting are these images
that Emerson reflected, "But alas I write my diagrams in Water."[8]

## DIAGRAMS OF GOD

December 26, 1835, Emerson wrote:

> There are two objects between which the mind vibrates like a pen-
> dulum; one, the desire of Truth; the other, the desire of Repose.
> He in whom the love of Repose predominates, will accept the first
> creed he meets, Arianism, Calvinism, Socinianism; he gets rest and
> reputation; but he shuts the door of Truth. He in whom the love
> of Truth predominates will keep himself aloof from all moorings

& afloat. He will abstain from dogmatism & recognize all the opposite negations between which as walls his being is swung. On one
side he will feel that God is impersonal. On the other, that the Universe is his work.[9]

Emerson had already resolved to avoid repose, that self-satisfied,
sometimes arrogant certainty that my way is *the* way and that success
lies in choosing a popular world-view. He was aware of that tendency
among the self-satisfied gentry of Boston, whose certainties made for
poor ground for fresh growth. We are reminded of the old priest who,
when asked if salvation was possible *outside* the Episcopal Church,
replied that although possible, it was not a path that a gentleman would
wish to take. Emerson's experience among what he referred to as "the
cultivated class" yielded this journal observation in May, 1836:

> And yet when cultivated men speak of God they demand a biog-
> raphy of him as steadily as the kitchen & the bar room demand
> personalities of men. Absolute goodness, absolute truth must leave
> their infinity & take form for us. We want fingers & sides & hair.
> Yet certainly it is more grand & therefore more true to say "Good-
> ness is its own reward"; "Be sure your sin will find you out," than
> to say God will give long life to the upright; God will punish the
> sinner in hell, in any popular sense of these words. But the angels
> will worship virtue & truth not gathered into a person but inly
> seen in the perspective of their own progressive being. They see
> the dream & the interpretation of the world in the faith that God
> is within them. As a spiritual truth needs no proof but is its own
> reason, so the Universe needs no outer cause but exists by its own
> perfection and the sum of it all is this, God is.[10]

This extensive passage contains much that is crucial to Emerson's
gathering perspectives and later work. Because the concept of the infinite allows facile imagery to enter our minds, we "gather" our
relationship to God in ideas of earthly authority. If, on the other hand,
we elevate our own sense of worth—note Emerson's use of the word
"angels" here—we are capable of taking responsibility in the moment
for our actions. This elevation is necessary in the removal of images of
personality in perceiving of God at all. It is part of the pendulum swing

of truth and repose. Also, here for the first time Emerson makes reference to the principle that a spiritual truth is its own evidence, a
philosophical assertion to which he will return again and again.

In addition, in choosing to use the assertion "God is . . ." Emerson
correctly evades the error of diminishing the word "God" by making it
the subject of a predicate such as love, great goodness, perfect, indeed
any number of such adjectives, which would render the word "God"
useless. If "God is love," for example, it is love that takes focus and
meaning. God becomes a weakened subject, removed grammatically
from centrality. Emerson's understanding of the power of language and
of its structure kept God always in the center of attention.

The thought enters Emerson's mind at this point to ask why we need
the idea or the name of God at all, particularly when we feel we can
envision a clockwork universe needing no maker.

> Theism must be & the name of God must be because it is a neces-
> sity of the human mind to apprehend the relative as flowing from
> the absolute & we shall always give the Absolute a name. But a
> storm of calumny will always pelt him whose view of God is high-
> est and purest.[11]

Religionists will argue that any image of God as Absolute in what
Emerson refers to as the highest and purist conception is the same as
atheism, and it was this whirlpool Emerson wished to avoid. Unless a
God is personal, they argue, in the sense of being an authority figure or
answerer of prayers, God is *in absentia*. Emerson's task was to attribute
qualities to a God who exists in active relation to the Universe and who
"embodies" in some sense the virtues of perfection. He approached that
task from two points: the nature of the Universe in the larger sense and,
second, the nature of the human mind in the narrow sense.

In a note which would later appear in "History," "Spiritual Laws,"
and "Demonology," Emerson establishes God's relationship to the
individual human mind:

> There is one Mind. Inspiration is larger reception of it: fanaticism
> is predominance of the individual. The greater genius the more
> like all other men, therefore. A man's call to do any particular work
> as to go super cargo to Calcutta, or missionary to Serampore, or

pioneer to the Western country is his fitness to do that thing he proposes. Any thought that he has a personal summons . . . is so much insanity. It denotes deficiency of perceiving that there is One Mind in all the individuals.[12]

Emerson's "angels" are those who understand that God does not speak to them in particulars—in dates, names, and places—but rather that the One Mind receives the same inspiration as pertaining to all of human life. We hear truths, not directions. Emerson had little patience with those who testify that God told them specifically to pack up and go to Africa to convert the "savages." What God did provide was a seed within the individual which would grow into talents, which in turn would speak to that person in terms of a calling in the world. We use the term God-given talents in this sense.

"God is the Universal Mind," Emerson says to conclude this journal entry, consciously placing the emphasis on Mind in his gathering vision.[13] His first, essential image of God comes then from pre-socratic sources. It comes from the Greek ideas of mind which connect the *Logos* of Heraclitus to the *Nous* of Anaxagoras, who saw *Nous* as the source of all order and life itself. These ideas of Mind are devoid of personality, and insofar as we can attune our minds to its operations, we take strength and inspiration from the connection. Emerson was playing with substitutions in the journal entries, trying to find an original, potent symbol for the Infinite.

It was at this time, in June of 1836, that Emerson was completing the text of *Nature*. In the bulk of the final chapter, "Prospects," Emerson deflects the text away from the production of ordinary prose by saying, "I shall therefore conclude this essay with some traditions of man and nature, which a certain poet sang to me."[14] His intent was to characterize this section of *Nature* with the elevated spirit of intuited inspiration.

The day before he began these last passages, he had taken a walk through the woods and pastures during a storm. Like Lear on the blasted heath, he was filled with the ambiguities of knowledge, feeling, and understanding. His perceptions both diminish and exalt him at the same time. The experience of that walk released in him a torrent of creative power not before seen, to which the last pages of Nature give their testimony. His journal describes the experience.

> Yesterday I walked in the storm. And truly in the fields I am not alone or unacknowledged. They nod to me & I to them. The waving of the boughs of trees in a storm is new to me & old. It takes me by surprise & yet is not unknown. Its effect is like that of a higher thought or a better emotion coming over me when I deemed I was thinking justly or doing right. We distrust & deny inwardly our own sympathy with nature. We own & disown our relation to it. We are like Nebuchadnezzer cast down from our throne bereft of our reason & eating grass like an ox.[15]

He refers to the effects of the storm in shaking him loose from Repose, that false feeling of satisfaction with the world, or the easy dependency upon traditional images. Nature, both in storm and calm, both in the close woods or the open fields, served to bring Emerson's mind to that new place where he could give accurate expression to spiritual truths. In choosing to live in Concord, he found conditions proper to his explorations, with its open fields, its placid river, its wooded hills and ponds, including Walden (to which he would eventually extend his property and loan Thoreau a small piece for his experiment in reflective isolation).

Images of nature keep connecting him to the process of perception in the mind.

> Respect yourself. You have first an instinct, then an opinion, then a knowledge, as the plant has root, bud, & fruit. Trust the instinct to the end, though you cannot tell why or see why. It is vain to hurry it. By trusting it, it shall ripen into thought & truth & you shall know why you believe.[16]

As his thought ripened, he began to refine his fundamental insights and to clarify how he would express them to the general public. First among these was the image of "The God Within," a central point of analysis for Emerson. Referring earlier to that trope as coming from the "spiritualist,"[17] he reflects upon the implications of the image some weeks later:

Observe this invincible tendency of the mind to unify. It is a law of our constitution that we should not contemplate things apart without the effort to arrange them in order with known facts & ascribe them to the same law. I do not choose to say, "God is within me—I do not like your picture of an external God. I suppose there is one spirit, & only one, the selfsame which I behold inly when I am overcome by an aweful moral sentiment and He made the world." I do not choose to say this. It is said for me by tyrannical instincts.[18]

To clarify, Emerson makes reference to these "tyrannical instincts" in "The American Scholar" when he describes the tendency toward a simplistic unifying of things as being the tendency of the young, presumably immature, mind. The entire passage continues the difficult process of coming to terms with what nature reveals and how the mind leaps at arranging these laws according to their own tendencies. The truth is not so much different as more complex, and Emerson was loath to accept an oversimplified image when a more accurate one could be found.

If, as he says, "The Universal law is the single fact,"[19] then an image which separates and delineates is false. To suggest that God is within, for example, immediately suggests its negating opposite. In answer to the child's question, "Where is God?," an answer that includes a place at once limits and excludes. How then are we to frame the idea of presence? One expression of a solution to the problem appears in the journal for October, 1836:

As long as the soul seeks an external God, it never can have peace, it always must be uncertain what may be done & what may become of it. But when it sees the Great God far within its own nature, then it sees that always itself is a party to all that can be, that always it will be informed of that which will happen and therefore it is pervaded with a great Peace.[20]

In giving character here to the soul doing the seeking, Emerson removes the tendency of the organizing intellect to leap to its unifying tendencies. The image of the soul perceiving "far within its own nature" to find God and, by extension, the Peace it perpetually seeks, helps to frame the nature of the forces at work. Two great questions are thus answered in this knowledge: What are the limits of my existence? and What is going to happen to me? Emerson frames such answers in terms of the soul's relationship to these questions, rather than the personality's more material ones. As he says in the next two sentences, "The individual is always dying. The Universal is life."[21]

Another glimpse of this question of presence appeared in the now famous Gospel According to Thomas, part of the Nag-Hammadi materials discovered in Upper Egypt in 1945. Although Emerson did not know of these materials, some light is shed on his unique vision of the "God Within" by one of Jesus' sayings in the text: "But the Kingdom is within you and it is without you. If you know yourselves, then you will know that you are the sons of the Living Father."[22]

## WHAT IS GOD?

This next question is posed as an exercise in abstract reasoning. After expressing the fundamental principle that "The All is in Man," Emerson lays out the ground of seeking for the nature of God. His first observation comes from the folk sayings of Vicesimus Knox, portions of whose *Elegant Extracts . . . in Prose* (London, 1797) Emerson had copied out on May 12, 1832.[23] On this occasion he begins his explorations into the nature of God with the image "God comes to see us without bell." This first idea clears away the need for intermediaries—including Jesus and the Church—in the individual's relationship with God and, more controversially, for personal revelation. The passage that follows spells out the image of the chasm of knowledge and in what manner the mind is able to grasp the Infinite.

> The walls are taken away; we lie open on one side to all the deeps of spiritual nature, to all the attributes of God. Justice we see and know; that is of God. Truth we see and know, that is of God. Love, Freedom, Power, these are of God. For all these & much more there is a general nature in which they inhere or of which they are phases and this is Spirit. It is essentially vital. The love that is in me,

the justice, the truth can never die & that is all of me that will not die. All the rest of me is so much death—my ignorance, my vice, my corporal pleasure. But I am nothing else than a capacity for justice, truth, love, freedom, power. I can imbibe them forevermore. They shall be so much to me that I am nothing, they all. Then shall God be all in all. Herein is my Immortality. And the soul affirms with the same assurance I shall live forever, as it affirms, Justice shall live forever.[24]

In order to know the ineffable, immeasurable God, we must have knowledge of these attributes: Justice, Truth, Love, Freedom, and Power. Our faculties of mind and our powers of observation allow us to perceive the actions of these attributes in the world, and insofar as we embody them, we are part of God. The key to the insight, however, and what carries it beyond a minor piece of abstracting, is the assertion that "it is essentially vital."

# 7    ATTRIBUTES OF GOD

*As we* have noted, following an argument through Emerson's formal writing takes us often along paths that seem to disappear into the wilderness. What seem like logical lines of inquiry are always vitalized by startling insights, what he himself called "lustres." To read Emerson is to enter a thick wood of abstract ideas and then discover that once we are inside these sanctuaries of spiritual nature, we encounter wild creatures that threaten our even, complacent perceptions. His art instigates rather than explains. To repeat, "It is essentially vital."

Such is the usefulness, then, in selecting a series of important terms—in this case, the attributes of God—to see how Emerson amplified them with lustres of instigation in his formal work. If God consists of the perfection of justice, truth, love, freedom, and power, we may be able to approach some understanding of that formulation by extending these terms as expressions of perfection. Our limited understanding of these terms defines our own human boundaries as we try to conceive of an idea of God. Plato's interest in defining Justice, for example, especially in the *Republic,* serves this same purpose. Plato was interested in perfect justice. As we shall see, Emerson's interest in him stems from this same method of inquiry into the nature of the Infinite, although Emerson's dialectic might be said to be a self-reflective dialogue between the transcendent seer and the pragmatic Yankee.

Before we examine these attributes in some depth, however, it will be instructive to examine a pivotal journal entry dated 14 February, 1839, to see how Emerson's grasp of human perception reveals the way we commonly think about deity. It is a revealing but difficult passage, and one that he chose not to use in his formal writings.

. . . The faith in a Genius; in a family Destiny; in a ghost; in an amulet; is the projection of that instinctive care which the individual takes of his individuality beyond what is meet & into the region where the individuality is forever bounded by generic, cosmic, & universal laws.

Yet I find traces of this usurpation in very high places, in Christianity for example. Christianity as it figures now in the history of ages intrudes the element of a limited personality into the high place which nothing but spiritual energy can fill, representing that Jesus can come in, where a will is an intrusion, into growth, repentance, reformation.

The divine will, or *the eternal tendency to the good of the whole, active in every atom, every moment,*—is the only will that can be supposed predominant a single hairbreadth beyond the lines of individual action & influence as known to experience; but a ghost, a Jupiter, a fairy, a devil, and not less a saint, an angel, & the God of popular religion, as of Calvinism, & Romanism, is an aggrandized & monstrous individual will. The divine will, such as I describe it, is spiritual. These other things, though called spiritual, are not so, but only demonological; & a fiction.[1]

This severe assessment of our popular religious myth-making makes the important point that in order for our own spiritual will to function properly, we cannot allow to intrude upon it another individualized will, a personification which speaks, or admonishes, or warns, even. Our own spiritual voice must be free to express itself, with eloquence, as we shall see in the next chapter. Emerson's own emphasis makes the central point, *that the eternal tendency to the good of the whole, active in every atom, every moment,* must be the only power acknowledged as we proceed toward our own fulfillment. If this is so, then the attributes of God described below will be the appropriate, vital forces active not only in every atom at every moment, but present as well in our own conscious awareness and being.

## INTIMATIONS OF TRUTH

It was Emerson's position that professional philosophy, at least in his era, was not in the truth-seeking business, but rather was devoted to system-building. His observation might have been a reaction to Hegel in particular. The matter of truth was too elusive, too much the province of the Infinite to come under the discipline of systematic analysis. In "Literary Ethics" he takes his stand.

> But, Truth is such a flyaway, such a slyboots, so untransportable and unbarrelable a commodity, that it is as bad to catch as light. Shut the shutters never so quick, to keep all the light in, it is all in vain; it is gone before you can cry, Hold. And so it happens with our philosophy. Translate, collate, distil all the systems, it steads you nothing; for truth will not be compelled, in any mechanical manner. But the first observation you make, in the sincere act of your nature, though on the veriest trifle, may open a new view of nature and of man, that, like a menstruum, shall dissolve all theories in it; shall take up Greece, Rome, Stoicism, Eclecticism, and what not, as mere data and food for analysis, and dispose of your world-containing system, as a very little unit. A profound thought, anywhere, classifies all things: a profound thought will lift Olympus.[2]

These images of truth, so offhand in their offering it seems, nonetheless make the point. From folk tale to economics to physics, truth is not to be cornered or even contained. It is as quick and elusive as light. And yet it is never, in Emerson's view, relative, never the possession of each person according to whim. Emerson's early declaration that he had never spoken the truth, read it, or heard it spoken placed its nature and quality at a goodly distance from individual human articulation. His position was that God is the Truth, is Reality, and that knowing the truth is the same as seeing God. Like Moses seeking truth, we might, if we are elected, catch a fleeting glimpse of a departing coat-tail. Such glimpses are not relative, but they also are not complete.

What then are the characteristics of truth caught in brief glimpses? In what way was it an attribute of God? How was it revealed? One characteristic symbol of truth in Emerson is that it is a foundation. Among its lesser attributes, truth was fundamental, primary. It supported the others. Another image, which we see in his journal for April, 1837, when he first was gathering images for the fundamental natures of God, is "capital stock." This image struck home at a time when America was in financial crisis. The bank failures of 1837, so disastrous for the country, had put pressure on Emerson. His small investments dried up, leaving him unable to meet expenses and obligations. But he was still solvent because he was not overextended. The journal entry for April reflects something of the times.

How wild & mysterious our position as individuals to the Universe! Here is always a certain amount of truth lodged as intrinsic foundation in the depths of the soul, a certain perception of absolute being, as justice, love, & the like, natures which must be the God of God, and this is our capital stock. This is our centripetal force. We can never quite doubt, we can never be adrift; we can never be nothing, because of this Holy of Holies, out of sight of which we cannot go.[3]

The entry ends with a reference to the abyss which always looms just before us, drawing us to its edge, not only in dreams but in ordinary affairs.

Then on the other side all is to seek. We understand nothing; our ignorance is abysmal,—the overhanging immensity staggers us, whither we go, what we do, who we are, we cannot even so much as guess. We stagger and grope.[4]

Here again is the image of the chasm which confronts us as seekers. On the human side, in life and in the mind, we see truth as a foundation to build upon or capital stock to be held in reserve, to support us, or as the force of gravity maintaining our place in the universe. On the other side, as spiritual seekers, all is darkness in which we perpetually grope toward the light.

The tendency to form images comes as much from the natural laws of the mind as it does from cultural influence. We have already heard Emerson warn that the lower faculties of mind leap too quickly to categorize, leaving us with what he would later call in "Worship" a "savage interpretation." What brings us close to the Infinite involves more hearing and seeing than speaking. When we receive the elements of truth out of nature, we come closer to understanding than if we form images in speech or writing—unless those images reflect, as much as possible, natural forces. For example:

> As long as I hear truth, I am bathed by a beautiful element & am not conscious of any limits to my nature. The suggestions are thousandfold that I hear & see. The waters of the great Deep have ingress and egress to the soul. But if I speak, then I define, confine, & am less. Silence is a menstruum that dissolves personality & gives us leave to be great & universal.[5]

Growing in Emerson increasingly was the perception that in describing the attributes of God, truth had to be expressed in images external to the human form and yet compatible with human experience. The dangers of image-making, however, are clear enough, and silence is a necessary solvent. The trick is to see in the image a shadow only and not the object itself. Danger lurks in looking too directly.

> Truth is our element & life, yet if a man fasten his attention upon a single aspect of truth, & apply himself to that alone for a long time, the truth itself becomes distorted, &, as it were, false. Herein resembling the air which is our natural element & the breath of the nostrils, but if a stream of air be directed upon the body for a time it causes cold, fever, even death.[6]

These passages have in common that they are in the form of warnings, clarifications, approaches, and are not definitions or philosophical statements. Emerson is at play in the world of symbols. Truth is air and water to us, giving us life, but we can also die from excess of either. Seeing truth, like seeing God, can be fatal. It is interesting, in the light of these images, that references to God's judgment appear to the cataclysmically inclined in disasters of wind and water. A recent example was reported in the aftermath of a tornado. A child looked at the rubble of his house and asked, "Why did God do this?"

In a late essay, "Immortality," found in *Letters and Social Aims*, Emerson returns truth to its abstract ground, as his final thought on the matter.

> Salt is a good preserver; cold is; but a truth cures the taint of mortality better, and "preserves from harm until another period." A

sort of absoluteness attends all perception of truth,—no smell of age, no hint of corruption. It is self-sufficing, sound, entire.

## JUSTICE

In the orthodox traditions, God's biblical justice is articulated in Judgments, from the expulsion from Eden to intimations of the final Apocalypse. In biblical imagery, our relationship to God is seen as master to servant and father to child. It is articulated through obedience to His Commandments, the forgiveness of sins, and the showering down of undeserved grace and mercy. Even in the case of Job, where God's punishment appears at first unjust and inexplicable, the message is that God's judgment is never to be questioned. Job's human understanding releases a diatribe against God's justice, which God answers within the Yahwist tradition:

> Brace yourself like a fighter,
>> now it is my turn to ask questions and yours to inform me.
> Do you really want to reverse my judgment,
>> and put me in the wrong to put yourself in the right?
> Has your arm the strength of God's,
>> can your voice thunder as loud?[7]

Here is the vision of the not so transcendent God characterized by the author of Job as being beyond judgment and human understanding in dispensing justice to human beings. What appears unjust to human perception, such as the loss of innocent life or the guilty living unpunished, is not to be questioned. Faith in God's eventual Judgment will have to do.

Emerson framed his own mystical vision in rebellion from this tradition. He powerfully set forth his objection to it in his essay "Compensation." His sarcasm in presenting the tradition leaps at the reader as he states his wish to correct the orthodox view.

> I was lately confirmed in these desires by hearing a sermon at church. The preacher, a man esteemed for his orthodoxy, unfolded in the ordinary manner the doctrine of the Last Judgment. He assumed, that judgment is not executed in this world; that

the wicked are successful; that the good are miserable; and then urged from reason and from Scripture a compensation to be made to both parties in the next life. No offence appeared to be taken by the congregation at this doctrine. As far as I could observe, when the meeting broke up, they separated without remark on the sermon.

He continues in his criticism by spelling out the extent of the problem and the source of its immediate correction:

The fallacy lay in the immense concession, that the bad are successful; that justice is not done now. The blindness of the preacher consisted in deferring to the base estimate of the market of what constitutes a manly success, instead of confronting and convicting the world from the truth; announcing the presence of the soul; the omnipotence of the will; and so establishing the standard of good and ill, of success and falsehood.

Emerson's proposal that divine justice is to be understood in the great law of compensation within the human soul is presented as a fusion of cause and effect taking place in the moment.

Crime and punishment grow out of one stem. Punishment is a fruit that unsuspected ripens within the flower of the pleasure which concealed it. Cause and effect, means and ends, seed and fruit, cannot be severed; for the effect already blooms in the cause, the end preexists in the means, the fruit in the seed.

Emerson affirms the vitality of perfect justice not just as an attribute of God but as a fixed attribute of the human condition.

Thus is the universe alive. All things are moral. That soul, which within us is a sentiment, outside of us is a law. We feel its inspiration; out there in history we can see its fatal strength. "It is in the world, and the world was made by it." Justice is not postponed. A perfect equity adjusts its balance in all parts of life.

Emerson's use of internal "sentiment" equated with external law, or the unity of subjective and objective in perception, is Kantian. Sentiment, or feeling, is equivalent to the German *Gefül* and relates to Kant's distinctions between pleasure and pain. For Kant, the feeling of plea-sure arises in the presence of harmony between an object and the subjective conditions of life and consciousness. Pain arises from the awareness of disharmony. For Emerson, the perception of feelings of peace and harmony was an indication of the sentiment of virtue in the presence of moral law.

Therefore, the images that begin to accumulate to define perfect jus-tice include balance and harmony, expressed in the image of water perfectly seeking its own level.

> There is a deeper fact in the soul than compensation, to wit, its own nature. The soul is not a compensation, but a life. The soul *is*. Under all this running sea of circumstance, whose waters ebb and flow with perfect balance, lies the aboriginal abyss of real Being. Essence, or God, is not a relation, or a part, but the whole.

Emerson uses the image of balance again in describing Plato as the perfectly balanced mind. The equation between perfect balance and justice reveals itself in the argument in the *Republic,* as Socrates walks the tightrope over the abyss of Being to arrive at a definition of Jus-tice. His conclusion, that " . . . the fairest fortune that can befall man is to be guided by his *daemon* to that which is truly his own"[8] makes the connection between justice and calling. For a human being, justice is served when we do our own work, with the first task, of course, of finding what it is that we are meant to do. Seen this way, all the agony, not to mention time and money, spent on discovering our true calling is primarily the search for justice within the soul. Why finding our true calling is so complex a problem is that, at bottom, the search is really a search for perfect justice and not merely for something to do. When we finally arrive at such a calling we can know it, therefore, by the feel-ing of balance and harmony that comes when we are doing the right work. Anything less tells us that the search has not ended.

Emerson's intention was to deflect the idea of justice away from ideas of retribution or more narrow concepts of compensation. When we seek justice in courts of law, suing for compensation for our per-ceived losses, it is only in the abstract that what we are truly seeking is balance and harmony. And yet the idea is still there. Legal compensation in the system of justice is designed to preserve social harmony and to restore balance to the social order.

As Emerson knew, distortion of the purity of that idea occurs when we attribute justice to a distant God whose retributions are executed in the hereafter. If human beings truly understood that human justice is to be found in each individual's discovery of his or her own proper work, and that to prevent other human beings from making that discovery or from doing their proper work constitutes injustice, we would have a much clearer vision of how to punish and subsequently reform offenders of that principle.

## LOVE

Plato employs the image of *eros* as the means by which the chasm between the human and divine realms is bridged. Emerson follows that example in equating love to the bridging power of a desirous consciousness. In the essay "Love," this Platonic connection is made in youthful passions. "The passion rebuilds the world for the youth. It makes all things alive and significant. Nature grows conscious." Love is the quality or substance which makes us aware that we are human beings. And that awareness is most clearly manifest to us in the presence of beauty—not the beauty of art, but the beauty of nature, including the human form.

Emerson's reflective consideration of beauty as an attribute of God appears in his journals during 1837, in this case juxtaposed to the observation that "The most tedious of all discourses are on the subject of the Supreme Being."9 His interest in the vitality essential to his subject takes form in this entry:

> Beauty is ever that divine thing the ancients esteemed it. It is, as they said "the flowering of Virtue." I see one & another, & another fair girl, about whose form or face glances a nameless charm. I am immediately touched with an emotion of tenderness or complacency. They pass on, and I stop to consider at what this dainty emotion, this wandering gleam points. It is no poor animal instinct, for this charm is destroyed for the imagination by any reference to

animalism. It points neither to any relations of friendship or love that society knows & has, but it seems to me to a quite other & now unattainable sphere, relations of transcendent delicacy & sweetness, a true faerieland to what roses & violets hint & fore-shadow. We cannot *get at* beauty. Its nature is evanescent.[10]

This April musing has about it a spring fancy, but underlying its sentiment is a connection he would continue to explore in all weathers. When Emerson indicates that he stopped to consider his feelings, we witness again the power love has to make conscious our presence in nature, which when combined with a sound intellect points to its transcendent effect. Later that year, in a more December mood, he spies another face and has a similar response.

The fair girl whom I saw in town expressing so decided & proud choice of influences, so careless of pleasing, so wilful & so lofty a will, inspires the wish to come nearer to & speak to this nobleness: So shall we be ennobled also. I wish to say to her, Never strike sail to any. Come into port greatly, or sail with God the seas. Not in vain you live, for the passing stranger is cheered, refined, & raised by a vision.[11]

This more physical beauty too reaches in eloquence the same level of perception. Although it may be more an image of courage (Emerson used the passage in "Heroism"), there resides in it the same adoration we found earlier.

The image reminds us of Dante's love for Beatrice, a subject to which Emerson was devoted in 1837 and again in 1844, when he completed an English translation of *La Vita Nuova*, Dante's poem devoted to Beatrice Portinari and written after her death in 1290. For Dante Alighieri and his friends, the transformation of Beatrice into an exemplar of divine love was part of their desire to awaken a quality of love close to God within the human soul. Once awakened, this quality would be the conduit to communion with the Divine Being. As an esoteric order the *fedeli d'amore*, as they called themselves, sought this union through the sentiments of love aroused in their Platonic adoration of women such as the idealized Beatrice.

Emerson's interest in this process of transformation had little to do with psychological sublimation of erotic desire. He simply examined, deeply, his perceptions of beauty in the women who passed through his life. Although his marriage to Lidia Jackson had less of the passion he felt for his first wife, Ellen Tucker, he understood the role of marriage as a spiritual union and was accepting of its workings upon him. Even Margaret Fuller's specific demands upon his affections were greeted by a cool courtesy she found infuriating, and his unwillingness to express greater personal affection dampened their friendship.

It was, in fact, Fuller who kept up the pressure on Emerson to translate Dante's *La Vita Nuova.* He would certainly not have done so merely as an exercise in improving his Italian, a passing knowledge of which he had gained during 1833. His real interest was in the subject of transformation and the relation between beauty, love, and divine knowledge. On three different occasions, Emerson made the following observation in his Topical Notebooks about *La Vita Nuova*:

> Dante's *Vita Nuova* reads like the Book of Genesis, as if written before literature, whilst truth yet existed. A few incidents are sufficient, & are displayed with oriental amplitude & leisure. It is the Bible of Love.[12]

Emerson's own experience and his work with Dante taught him that the transforming power of love manifests in the lover as a fresh and immediate gift of insight. Love makes us wise, not the reverse. In its maturity love gives strength to our intuitive powers, not blindness. Insofar as we love we come closest to the divine.

### POWER

After *Nature,* in which the word "power" appears so often (more than thirty times), we understand finally that his little book is centrally about restoring spiritual power to the fallen human condition. So ubiquitous are references to power in Emerson's thinking that his Idealism can finally be called a Vision of Power. In terms of the attributes of God, infinite power is our measure of what a god is. The questions for Emerson are What is the nature of this infinite power and How do human beings connect to that power.

Following are images of power found in *Nature.* In the first instance, we approach power as an exercise of the will, not dealing directly with its force but with its lessons. In Emerson's prose, balances are often struck as ratios, as in this case where "exercise" of the will is a "lesson" of power.

> The exercise of the Will or the lesson of power is taught in every event. From the child's successive possession of his several senses up to the hour when he saith, "Thy will be done!" he is learning the secret, that he can reduce under his will, not only particular events, but great classes, nay the whole series of events, and so conform all facts to his character.

Therefore, to the extent that our character is expansive, we have the power to conform facts to an expanding vision of reality. Next, from the other side of the chasm of knowing, power is presented as a Biblical fountain at which humanity is nourished, as in the valley of the shadow of death where the cup flows over in abundance. The distinction Emerson draws in this example is that God's power is not merely protective but is made overtly available for use.

> . . . the Supreme Being, does not build up nature around us, but puts it forth through us, as the life of the tree puts forth new branches and leaves through the pores of the old. As a plant upon the earth, so a man rests upon the bosom of God; he is nourished by unfailing fountains, and draws, at his need, inexhaustible power . . .

The source of this power for human beings rises up through Instinct and is therefore to be drawn with the intuitive faculty.

> He perceives that if his law is still paramount, if still he have elemental power, if his word is sterling yet in nature, it is not conscious power, it is not inferior but superior to his will. It is Instinct.

Emerson's use of the term "instinct" has been the subject of numerous studies. Essentially, human instinct for Emerson goes well beyond the exercise of the autonomic nervous system or DNA-driven behaviors. Instinct is the subconscious mind connected through human nature to the Universal Mind or Over-Soul. It is our source of movement across the abyss of spiritual knowledge, and it is also a power. The confusion of terminology comes when Emerson also connects Instinct to Reason, that aspect of Mind which provides understanding to the intellect.

In our post-Freudian, reductive view of human mental capacities, we tend to equate the subconscious with selfish desires and survival drives, reason with deliberate problem-solving, and instinct with preset biological programming. These definitions were also part of the materialistic world-view in Emerson's time, and it was against these reductions that *Nature* was written. As seen in *Nature* the result of the human instinctive grasp of God's being through Reason takes human perception beyond ordinary limits into the infinite.

> These are examples of Reason's momentary grasp of the sceptre; the exertions of a power which exists not in time or space, but an instantaneous in-streaming causing power.

In his series of essays gathered under the title *Conduct of Life*, given as lectures in the 1850s and published in 1860, there is an essay entitled "Power." In it Emerson deflects attention to what he calls "sublime considerations" to the essays on "Worship" and "Culture." This deflection is just like him, coming at a subject from an angle to get the best light on it. As the great Heraclitus said, "Nature prefers to hide."

He does offer, however, in "Power," an insight to which we may apply an interest in divine attributes:

> But this force or spirit, being the means relied on by Nature for bringing the work of the day about,—as far as we attach importance to household life, and the prizes of the world, we must respect that. And I hold, that an economy may be applied to it; it is as much a subject of exact law and arithmetic as fluids and gases are; it may be husbanded, or wasted; every man is efficient only as he is a container or vessel of this force, and never was any signal act or achievement in history, but by this expenditure.

We may understand the nature of power from the scientific laws of energy, about which we grow daily more and more sophisticated. Discovery of the laws of nuclear energy has supplanted the classical

laws of conservation in our laboratories. Our concerns now center on
containing immense power rather than conserving limited power. In
terms of potential destruction, we are as gods.

Emerson's description of Deity in "Worship" takes the deflected form
of principle and presence while opposing the formula of the God Within so commonly attributed to him. In the following passage from that
essay, he spells out his sense of the relationship to make clear where
the power he is speaking of finally resides.

> There is a principle which is the basis of things, which all speech
> aims to say, and all action to evolve, a simple, quiet, undescribed,
> undescribable presence, dwelling very peacefully in us, our right-
> ful lord: we are not to do, but to let do; not to work, but to be
> worked upon; and to this homage there is a consent of all thought-
> ful and just men in all ages and conditions. To this sentiment
> belong vast and sudden enlargements of power.

The great stream of power emanating from God flows through and
around us, like cosmic rays flowing through us every moment. Our
proper task, Emerson affirms, is—through our reflective powers in
mind—to allow ourselves enough obedience to be a witness to and an
instrument of this subtle power. The soul dwells within us as a presence. We gather to us the emanating power that surrounds us in order
to empower the soul.

## FREEDOM

A tension always exists in Emerson between freedom and this necessary obedience. His over-arching term is "a necessitated freedom."
Over-riding that tension, however, is always the presence of an early
affirmation of fundamental freedom away from which he never strayed
far. We see again, from his journal for December 21, 1823, this eloquent
paean to the sublime:

> Who is he that shall control me? Why may not I act & speak &
> think with entire freedom? What am I to the universe, or, the
> Universe, what is it to me? Who hath forged the chains of
> Wrong & Right, of Opinion and Custom? And must I wear them?

Is society my anointed King? Or is there any mightier community or any man or more than man, whose slave I am? I am solitary
in the vast society of beings; I consort with no species; I indulge
no sympathies. I see the world, human, brute & inanimate nature;
I am in the midst of them, but not of them; I hear the sound of
the storm,—the Winds & warring Elements sweep by me—but
they mix not with my being. I see cities & nations & witness passions,—the roar of their laughter,—but I partake it not;—the yell
of their grief,—it touches no chord in me; their fellowships &
fashions, lusts and virtues, the words & deeds they call glory and
shame,—I disclaim them all. I say to the Universe, Mighty one!
thou art not my mother; Return to chaos, if thou wilt, I shall still
exist. I live. If I owe my being, it is to a destiny greater than thine.
Star by Star, world by world, system by system shall be crushed,
—but I shall live.[13]

Emerson made the more prosaic statement much later that his body
was the office where he worked. This detachment, placing the "I" in the
living, infinite spaces of the Godhead, separate from matter, decay, and
change, places Emerson in an irreconcilable world of philosophical
dualism characteristic of many Neoplatonists. And yet—and the excep-
tion was forever his impulse—his inspired thought emerged from a
fundamental perception of unity. It was as if the forces that confined
him to mortality faded into insignificance when his idealism called,
even in the darkest hours, such as when Ellen or his son Waldo died.

In his lecture "Religion," which he first delivered in Boston during
1839–40 in the series *The Present Age*, Emerson set forth vigorous expressions of the Godhead to correspond to his more abstract attributes,
including freedom, which conform to universal laws.

How can it be that this eternal nature, this Oversoul, the supreme
fact, should never in the circling ages find an adequate expression
in the world? that the Godhead who does not dwell neither in mul-
titudes neither in chosen men but in every man—who is made
apparent never in personal attributes but ever in sublime universal laws should not be worshipped purely in them?[14]

The second question in this passage is more than merely rhetorical. The universal laws, including love, justice, power, truth, and freedom, approach human understanding and are innate in the untapped intellect. They are attributes of the entity called God and express themselves in daily life as well as in historical eras. Inasmuch as "God" is unknowable except through attributes, it is these that govern our knowledge, as mentioned in the previous chapter. The error, semantically, is to say, "God is love" or "God is justice," thus reducing the image "God" to a weak subject and throwing the matter of attribute onto a predicate.

As opposed to many "men of faith," Emerson was comfortable with skepticism. His doubt was not, however, founded on questioning what his own perceptions of the truth had revealed to him. It had its source in what forms were yet to be revealed. In the case of the two questions posed in the passage above, he offered the following answer:

> If this age is called skeptical it is because it loves this truth. If the heart beats with this immense private hope will not another age find modes to embody the faith.[15]

"This truth" refers to the principle of the Godhead who is revealed and whose nature rests in sublime universal laws, and to the degree that we understand those laws we understand God, and to the degree that we embody those laws we speak and act for God in the world.

# 8
# THE CONSCIOUS
# HUMAN BEING

*As readers* of Emerson know well, his central image of the evolved human being is *Man Thinking.* It emerged in "The American Scholar," a speech he delivered as the Phi Beta Kappa Address in Cambridge in 1837, a year prior to the "Address." For Emerson, Man Thinking was the philosophical extension of the scholar living the examined life. Ideally this would be a person of reflective skill and instinctive action, casting a long shadow over the wilderness of the American continent. The image was of Realized Man, Conscious Man, Idealized Man. Today, with proper concern for gender-inclusive language, we would say the Conscious Individual, in which the term "conscious" implies a reflective self-awareness.

The present incarnation of the image has less of the scholar and more of the interactive, spiritual human being. We envision a person evolved to the point of understanding Plato's *examined life,* existence without which, as Socrates said, is not worth having.

In a real sense, Emerson's speech at Cambridge that late summer day in 1837 was a failure, at least philosophically. Taken merely as America's "intellectual declaration of independence" by Oliver Wendell Holmes and others present that day, the central point of the speech was lost on most of the listeners, at least on those dedicated to the traditional role of the scholar in a traditional social and religious society.

Emerson's philosophical point had been very different than what Holmes celebrated. It was an extension of the thought in *Nature,* a call for the virtues of the consciously examined life based on the principle that human beings have access to the One Mind, which is the Divine Mind, and that we are capable of consciously reflecting that mind uniquely with our individual lives. The idea of the One Mind is not equivalent to Jung's Collective Unconscious taken as racial memory. Neither is it what we might today call the vestiges of evolutionary development encoded in DNA and passed along to our unconscious behaviors. Rather, the One Mind, or Over-Soul, is a pervasive substance of the universe having attributes of divine will perceived by human understanding as universal law. This principle animates the most powerful of the passages in "The American Scholar":

> The world,—this shadow of the soul, or *other me*, lies wide around. Its attractions are the keys which unlock my thoughts and make me acquainted with myself. I run eagerly into this resounding tumult. I grasp the hands of those next me, and take my place in the ring to suffer and to work, taught by an instinct, that so shall the dumb abyss be vocal with speech. I pierce its order; I dissipate its fear; I dispose of it within the circuit of my expanding life. So much only of life as I know by experience, so much of the wilderness have I vanquished and planted, or so far have I extended my being, my dominion. I do not see how any man can afford, for the sake of his nerves and his nap, to spare any action in which he can partake. It is pearls and rubies to his discourse. Drudgery, calamity, exasperation, want, are instructors in eloquence and wisdom. The true scholar grudges every opportunity of action past by, as a loss of power.

First, rather than speak to the "Flatland" of traditional values represented by this Harvard and Boston gathering, Emerson evoked the "dumb abyss" over which he urged his audience to reach. He truly intended, as he said, to "dispose of it within the circuit of my expanding life." To do so meant that he had to make a case for an authentic capacity within the human being to vault that chasm with innate but as yet unrealized resources, and to do so in this lifetime.

The first of the capacities needed in this process was in evidence, and it was the eloquence of the address itself. "The high prize of eloquence may be mine," he had written in his journal in 1834.[1] He was not speaking merely of a talent, but rather of that resource of the spirit that might capture images of the truth under the influence of inspiration. Eloquence is evidence of right listening and effective translation across the abyss of nature, and it is particularly evident in those who draw from the reservoir of personal experience. It is not to be confused with sophistry, that exercise of gesture and voice aimed at persuasion. True eloquence is truth washing up against the hardened layers of illusion and habit, which are built up around us from years of habitual repose.

"The American Scholar" was an auspicious beginning in the public eye for Emerson. The impression he made that day was the signal of his emergence. It marked the beginning of his primary work as a speaker, essayist, and poet: the expansion of the range of consciousness within the human being, or as he had it in a later 1840 journal entry, "the infinitude of the private man."[2] It was also the emergence of an important independent individual, unattached and free from obligation to any institution or party.

In 1838, after the infamy and notoriety of the "Divinity College Address," Emerson made the decision late in the year to no longer fill pulpits as a guest preacher. He gave up sermonizing and confined his lecturing to the lyceum circuit. As we see in the journals after 1838, his primary interest shifted away from theology *per se* and concentrated on the potential genius of human nature. He had scanned the horizon over the chasm between the divine and human worlds and had done his best to describe what he saw there. The attributes of God described in chapter seven were what rose to greet his rational and reflective human perception. No myths or sentimental personifications could or should fill the intervening gulf. The next task was to discover and describe the capacities of divinity in human character.

We begin this exploration with the warning from G.K. Chesterton, who remarked that "the most horrible is the worship of the god within. . . . That Jones shall worship the god within him turns out ultimately to mean that Jones shall worship Jones." Emerson knew perfectly well what his critics have forgotten in their claims of heresy:

that the *knowledge* of the Infinite resides within the human instrument.

When Emerson qualified the idea of the "God Within" as he did, he chose not to use the term as adequate to describe human nature except as "deeply within the soul of Man." Instead of exalting that idea, he began to confront reductionist images of traditional Calvinism and scientific materialism, both of which seriously diminished human potential and what he called "the erect position." His original image from *Nature* of the human being as a god in ruins was aimed as much at contemporary scientific thinking as at human historical and theological failure.

The force of the materialist view was being demonstrated in England by another writer in the same period. The opposing voice was so powerful as to assume vast historical influence over the next century and a half. The sound of the articulation remains compelling even today:

> In direct contrast to German philosophy which descends from heaven to earth, here we ascend from earth to heaven. That is to say, we do not set out from what men say, imagine, conceive, nor from men as narrated, thought of, imagined, conceived, in order to arrive at men in the flesh. We set out from real, active men, and on the basis of their real life-process we demonstrate the development of the ideological reflexes and the echoes of this life-process. The phantoms formed in the human brain are also, necessarily, sublimates of their material life-processes, which is empirically verifiable and bound to material premises. Morality, religion, metaphysics, all the rest of ideology and their corresponding forms of consciousness, thus no longer retain the semblance of independence. They have no history, no development; but men, developing their material intercourse, alter, along with this their real existence, their thinking and the products of their thinking. Life is not determined by consciousness, but consciousness by life.[3]

Here is the young Karl Marx standing idealism on its head. Sense-based and class-driven, Marx represented the strongest of early materialist thinking, here writing around 1844. Emerson's urgent task

was to counteract this rhetoric, so powerful and compelling, by mini-
mizing traditional hierarchal rhetoric—the aristocracy trying to
maintain its dominant place in society—and replacing it with a new
democratic articulation of the human being in nature, drawing upon
images based on common experience and yet with infinite import.

Marx asserted that idealism is a phantom formed in the human
brain. How could Emerson prove him wrong? What about an exalted
human potential can be shown to be real and in the nature of things?
Marx was fighting against assumptions about the divine right of kings
and the privileges of the upper classes which, as he saw it, confined the
masses to the status of beasts of burden. Divine Right of Place had been
one of the rights of ancient hierarchies and their impositions of divine
order upon human experience to their own private ends. In the aftermath of the American and French Revolutions, and in anticipation of
further movements of equality which would erupt and collapse in chaos
after 1848, Marx was articulating the new materialist vision of history
in the service of economic justice.

Emerson would not become acquainted with Marx until 1853, when
he read a piece entitled "Forced Emigration" in the *New York Tribune*
in which Marx attacked the modern means of production and their
effects on the worker. By then, the issues involved were economic and
less metaphysical. In the 1840s, however, rural America had yet to face
what was shaking England to its royal knees. In Concord Emerson was
concerned, as he had been for a decade, to show the spiritual reality
behind every natural (i.e., material) fact. Opposing the materialist
position, he proclaimed that every event has its generation in Spirit.
By Spirit here, he meant a causal background in which the subtle consciousness of God, through lawful principles established at creation,
works out destiny with the active participation of human will and
natural power. In this light, personal *freedom* and economic *justice*
would prevail.

It is certainly true that Emerson had his own Divine Right of Place
in the human hierarchy. His aristocracy was one of the spirit and made
up of the "Awakened Ones." This image came from the Greeks, specifically from Plato as articulated in the Thomas Taylor translations of

*Emerson's study, seen much as it was left in 1882*

1803, which Emerson had been studying since college days. Alongside Taylor's Plato in Emerson's study were Heraclitus, Hermes (the Hermetic tradition), Empedocles, and most importantly Plotinus. These texts all espouse the top-down hierarchy of emanation from the Divine Source into multiplicity, including nature. As Emerson expressed the principle in his journals: "Let a man not resist the law of his mind & he will be filled with the divinity which flows through all things."[4]

Emerson's notion of spiritual aristocracy is not based on birth or genetic talents, but on an aptness to receive the emanations from the Over-Soul: Candidacy for such reception is probably determined by natural law rather than by ambition or accident; this natural aristocracy exists in the nature of emanation itself; from the One come emanations to the Few, who in turn speak to and for the Many; from this emanation the Many evolve; the movement is circular.

This spiritual influx, however, is an ubiquitous divine flowing. It by no means restricts itself to certain specified individuals, groups, or races. It is equally available to all, with only this caveat: The gates of understanding must stand open through conscious effort, and the individual must be prepared by virtue of great powers of discrimination.

The first step in this gnostic influx is a subtle but crucial shift in perception. We are not to seek the divine externally, especially in mythic personality. We are rather to seek it deep within, at a point or place where the personal ego does not exert control over image-making. The first identification, then, is impersonal, without identity. It arises as a feeling, most closely associated with warmth and light, and further identified as well-being. Emerson's own moment of gnosis came with the famous "Transparent Eyeball" experience, lifted into eloquence in *Nature*.

> Standing on the bare ground,—my head bathed by the blithe air, and uplifted into infinite space,—all mean egotism vanishes. I become a transparent eye-ball; I am nothing; I see all; the currents of the Universal Being circulate through me; I am part or particle of God.

The vanishing of "mean egotism," or that diminished personality which acts in its own interests, comes first, prior to the gnostic infusion. First "we" disappear, and then the Lord enters.

Just as the attributes of God are revealed without "person," so too the human being receives them without "person." The bridge over the abyss will not carry the weight of personality; rather, it is traversed in the mind's transparent (disembodied) eye. As such, no proof of the existence of the bridge, or of God, or of the divine nature within, can be offered in sensory terms. When Emerson asserts that all spiritual truths are their own evidence, he is affirming the principle that a spiritual experience is in and of itself a proof. Such is the definition of "experiences." It is the essence of his idealism.

## REPRESENTATIVES

When Emerson offers his spiritual "proofs" of the "infinitude of the private man," he does so initially by example in the lives of genius, and then in the personal, more direct observations that arise in his own experience. These two methods often operate simultaneously so that the genius of a Plato, Shakespeare, or Montaigne is seen through a distinctive Emersonian lens, and is therefore never mere biography. The great geniuses of history, art, science, and philosophy embody universal principles and are to be used as such, not celebrated as mere personalities or exceptions to the common strain of human life. This principle is set forth in the introduction to "Representative Men," the essays Emerson devoted to the innate spiritual powers of the human being. This introduction, "The Uses of Great Men," is sometimes offered as a separate essay, but it is generally unread in the Emerson canon. In it he wrote,

> The genius of humanity is the real subject whose biography is written in our annals. We must infer much, and supply many chasms in the record. The history of the universe is symptomatic, and life is mnemonical. No man, in all the procession of famous men, is reason or illumination or that essence we were looking for; but is an exhibition, in some quarter, of new possibilities. Could we one day complete the immense figure which these flagrant points compose! The study of many individuals leads us to an elemental region wherein the individual is lost, or wherein all touch by their summits. Thought and feeling that break out there cannot be impounded by any fence of personality. This is the key to the power of the greatest men,—their spirit diffuses itself. A new quality of mind travels by night and by day, in concentric circles from its origin, and publishes itself by unknown methods: the union of all minds appears intimate; what gets admission to one, cannot be kept out of any other; the smallest acquisition of truth or of energy, in any quarter, is so much good to the commonwealth of souls.

If we are to understand history from this perspective, we must see events that are generated by personalities as symptomatic of the movements of the One Mind exhibited in each actor.

From the earliest journals in 1819, Emerson had been interested in fame, both his own potential and in the record of those who had achieved it. By 1845, after publishing two volumes of essays that undertook to define the infinitude of the self-reliant human being, he began to assemble what he referred to as his "representative men." His aim was to inscribe as complete an arc as possible around the central figure of the ideal of realized infinitude, his Man Thinking. His selection would include the philosopher, the poet, the skeptic, the mystic, the writer, and the man of action. He could have included the painter as well, and his choice would probably have been Michelangelo. Had he included the saint, Jesus would have been his natural choice. His thoughts on the latter were summed up in a journal entry in which he had made his final list: Plato, Shakespeare, Montaigne, Swedenborg, Goethe, and Napoleon Bonaparte. About Jesus he said:

> Jesus should properly be one head, but it requires great power of intellect & of sentiment to subdue the biases of the mind of the age, and render historic justice to the world's chief saint.[5]

Thoreau had urged Emerson to include Jesus, arguing that as a representative of the divine infusion leading to greatness no other human being stood as high as Jesus; but Emerson stood by his choices. Fortunately for our curiosity in the matter, however, we have in the journal for 1839 as complete an examination of the issue as we might hope to find short of a full essay.

The first offering begins with an example of what he later called (above) "the mind of the age," with reference to the role of Christianity.

> The whole world is in conspiracy against itself in religious matters. The best experience is beggarly when compared with the immense possibilities of man. Divine as the life of Jesus is, what an outrage to represent it as tantamount to the Universe! To seize one accidental good man that happened to exist somewhere at some time and say to the new born soul, Behold thy pattern; aim no longer to possess entire Nature, to fill the horizon, to fill the infinite amplitude of being with great life, to be in sympathy & relation with all creatures, to lose all privateness by sharing all natural action, shining with the Day, undulating with the Sea, growing with the tree, instinctive with the animals, entranced in beatific vision with the human reason. Renounce a life so broad & deep as a pretty dream & go in harness of that past individual, assume his manners, speak his speech,—this is the madness of Christendom.[6]

Nowhere else in the Works or the journals do we have such a clear statement of the strictures of historical Christianity upon human freedom. I am reminded of a large sign that was posted for years outside a Baptist church in New York City. It read, "Christ died for you. What have you done for Him lately?" Such impositions of "pattern" upon the growing soul not only stunt possibilities and the wonders of unique genius, but also create an impossible demand upon individual consciousness and action.

The journal entry goes on to describe the growth of the individual soul relieved of such an imposition.

> The soul always believes in itself. It affirms the Eternity & Omnipresence of God which these [insane usurpers] deny. It knows that all which has ever been is now—that the total world is my inheritance, & the life of all beings I am to take up into mine. By lowly listening omniscience is for me. By faithful receiving omnipotence is for me. But the way of the soul into its heaven is not to man but from man. It leaves every form of life & doctrine that ever existed. It touches no book or rite or crutch or guide or mediator; it gives itself alone, original, pure to the Lonely, Original, & Pure who on that condition inhabits, leads, & speaks through it. Then it is glad, young, & nimble. It is not wise but it sees thro' all things. IT is called religious but it is innocent. It calls the Light its own & shares the pleasures of all creatures. It plays evermore.[7]

This necessary freedom in the soul's venture into the world and into its heaven was Emerson's severe demand upon the religious experience. Nothing less would do. He had to be free to do anything in general in order to choose not to do something in particular. He had to be free of guides and mediators in order to approach God freely, which meant without personality, especially the historically imposed personality of Jesus. Such severity was, he knew, both difficult and dangerous. Without mediation, without the wise counsel of priests, how would the individual make his or her way? Caught between his instincts and his judgment, Emerson chose not to speak formally about this extremity of his conviction.

Still, here was the crux of the problem for the would-be conscious human being: How to proceed without following, How to make a new path in a new world without seeming to follow in the footsteps of these representatives? The danger of independence lay in gross egotism, shutting off the heart's access to connection in the isolating wilderness. It is comforting to have a path to follow; it suggests some tradition, some other wanderer making the same effort, and it suggests the presence of a goal at the end of the journey. The tradition of the guru has great appeal and practical application. We recall that Emerson, as a young man, had yearned for a teacher.

Emerson expressed his awareness of the dangers of his idealism in the same journal entry. He went on:

> And yet I know the dangers of this sort of speculation. It is somewhat not wholesome to be said in a detached form. It is not good to say with too much precision & emphasis that we are encroached upon by the claims of Jesus in the current theology. It brings us into a cold denying irreligious state of mind. It is of no use to *say,* Quit Jesus & the saints & heroes. But without the *saying* which is proud & so suicidal, let us turn our eyes to the Vast, the Good, the Eternal. There fasten the Eyes, there build the perpetual hearth & house & altar of the soul & dare to try thy pinions by flights into the Transcendent & Unknown. Thou awful Cause! hardly with sincerity can I ask that my eye may learn to keep upward, so prone is it ever to things around and below.[8]

It is weakness, then? Can we not forgo the deadly past and make bold steps into the Transcendent and Unknown? This abyss yawns forever before the human condition, asking for courageous crossing but chilling the heart with its dark, frightening depths. And yet—and here Emerson takes his stand—how can he sincerely ask God to help him keep his eye off the abyss when his constitution fixes his attention on its expanse? Perhaps here is a way, Emerson thought, in which the life and words of saints can serve us yet. The journal entry ends with an attempt at unity, some synthesis of the need for absolute freedom and the life of the sainted ones who have gone before.

> I was about to say & omitted it in the middle of the last page,— that we have nothing to do with Jesus in our progress, nothing to do with any past soul. The only way in which the life of Jesus or other holy person helps us is this, that as we advance without reference to persons on a new, unknown, sublime path, we at each

new ascent verify the experiences of Jesus & such souls as have obeyed God before. We take up into our proper life at that moment his act & word & do not copy Jesus but really *are* Jesus, just as Jesus in that moment of his life was us. Say, rather, it was neither him nor us, but a man at this & that time saw the truth & was transformed into its likeness.[9]

At each step in the process of discovering the role a human being will play in obeying the soul's destiny, whatever that might ultimately be, we return again to the attributes of God—the infinities of power, freedom, truth, love, justice—and begin to approach their likeness in human life. Transforming into the proper likeness of the truth is such an application and is a way of integrating the life of Jesus into our own authentic experience of "each new ascent."

## JESUS STUDIES

A glance at the present state of religious study devoted to the life and words of Jesus of Nazareth reveals a ground which is in some degree prepared for Emerson's severe demands. Theological movements such as The Jesus Seminar[10] and similar academic research efforts into biblical history have made an intellectually presentable case for millions of believers in God to the effect that Jesus was a man and not God, and that he was a remarkable teacher, prophet, and seer whose wisdom deserves devoted attention but not worship as a divinity.

The effect of this liberal remaking of the Christian mythus cancels the assertions of the Nicene Creed, the wording of which has been central to Christianity since it was formulated and adopted in 325 C.E. and revised in 381 and again in 589. The central premise adopted by the Council of Nicea was to make the Son "consubstantial" with the Father. The creed substituted the Greek word *homoousios,* the *same* substance, for *homoiousian,* of *like* substance.

What if, however, we consider that the aim of spiritual development or progress toward spiritual transformation entails a movement in the direction of a bodily transformation as well as a psychic or psychological transformation? Certainly the disciplines practiced by Eastern yogis have that goal, the end result of which could be characterized as *homoousios* in relation to the Absolute or Causal force of the universe.[11] Emerson's image of the spilling of the water of individuality into the great waters of divine Unity has that identity of "like substance," but at the level of mind only. The rest, as Emerson said, is so much death.

If Jesus had achieved in his lifetime that physical as well as psychic transformation, would he have achieved what the Nicene Creed asserted on his behalf? The words from the Gospel of Saint John from Chapter 17, the "priestly prayer of Christ," have this meaning and articulate the essential unity with the Father implicit in the Greek term *homoousios.* That Emerson wished to find a way to achieve that identity for Jesus seems clear. But as his comments imply, he knew that Jesus as a model who was *not* to be followed and yet still to serve as a distant archetype was a refinement too exacting for most Christians.

In this more abstract and theological sense, *Representative Men* remains unsatisfactory in achieving Emerson's lofty intent. The eloquence on behalf of Goethe, Shakespeare, and Swedenborg, to name three of the more successful essays, still fails to reach the heights intended. The essay on Plato, who achieved something of the sublime genius hinted at in "The Uses of Great Men," reflects the pattern of Emerson's effort. He says about Plato's influence:

> He stands between the truth and every man's mind, and has almost impressed language and the primary forms of thought with his name and seal.

The falling off of "almost" in that sentence indicates the problem of trying to recast the biographies of historical figures. We are too skeptical to attribute to personalities the status of receivers of revelation, hence our continuing adoration of Jesus in his mythic status as an exemplar without peer. The problem for Emerson became how to present the ideal of the conscious human being reaching into the infinite, while at the same time describing the complexities of the process without also affirming its inherent difficulties.

# 9  LIMITATION AND GENIUS

*The following* passage is from "The Editors to the Reader" of *The Dial*, the new venture initiated by Margaret Fuller and edited in its early numbers by Fuller and then Emerson. It seeks to characterize the potential readers of the new intellectual journal. Seen as part of a spiritual revolution, the army Emerson describes is at best a rag-tag group.

No one can converse much with different classes of society in New England, without remarking the progress of a revolution. Those who share in it have no external organization, no badge, no creed, no name. They do not vote, or print, or even meet together. They do not know each other's faces or names. They are united only in a common love of truth, and love of its work. They are of all conditions and constitutions. Of these acolytes, if some are happily born and well bred, many are no doubt ill dressed, ill placed, ill made—with as many scars of hereditary vice as other men. Without pomp, without trumpet, in lonely and obscure places, in solitude, in servitude, in compunctions and privations, trudging beside the team in the dusty road, or drudging a hireling in other men's cornfields, schoolmasters, who teach a few children rudiments for a pittance, ministers of small parishes of the obscurer sects, lone women in dependent condition, matrons and young maidens, rich and poor, beautiful and hard-favored, without concert or proclamation of any kind, they have silently given in their several adherence to a new hope, and in all companies do signify a greater trust in the nature and resources of man, than the laws or the popular opinions will well allow.[1]

This adverse Romanticism, first penned in the journals for September, 1839,[2] employs an image of this revolution in seeking as "a new hope." In editing the journal entry for *The Dial,* Emerson added the last three lines, expressing as a hope this having trust in the true nature and resources of the human being. Most of the journals after 1838 contain references to the limitations of the human condition, outlining in sometimes blunt frankness the failings of himself, family, friends, and strangers in their effort to absorb the "newness" of idealism as a practice. Certainly Emerson could never be accused of sentimentality when it came to human weakness. Continually finding himself in what he called the prone position, he nonetheless sought in life and eloquence to stand erect, to represent the spiritual reality of the human condition.

Even granting the difficulty of trying to describe the company that might find *The Dial* a valuable resource, Emerson's introduction falls short of inspiration because it focuses too much on limitation and too little on potential. Granted we are grounded to a fault by the forces that keep us mired in banality. Most religions remind us of these weaknesses *ad nauseam.* We do not expect Emerson to follow suit. So, what was his intent?

What we are witnessing in passages like this one is camouflage, the addition of protective coloring to those who are venturing unarmed into the wilderness on the transcendental path. Emerson was a nurturing figure in this new movement. He instinctively spread his protective wings over his brood, knowing how vulnerable they were to the gossip of traditional society and to the temptations of the extremes. After his Divinity College experience, he remained wary. He and his friends would proceed "without concert or proclamation" to seek the truth. In limitation and genius they would find their own solitary way. In that sense, the life of Henry Thoreau serves as a fitting example.

What drew all these like figures together was the conviction among them that the life of the mind is the central fact of human existence. It was also more than conviction, finally. Life was for them an ongoing discovery of the essential fact that human beings possess a mind and can live successfully according to its revealed laws, rather than according to the dictates of any external authority or set of opinions. The mind awake was the ultimate goal and reality to be sought and nurtured.

By the 1840s Emerson was on his way to establishing what we can call a science of mind. This was no easy matter after Kant, whose investigations of mind had drawn strict limitations around the capacities of the faculty of reason to affirm the existence of transcendental entities such as God and the human soul. In fact Kant had ultimately denied the possibility of a proper science of mind, at least as it pertains to the usual investigations of metaphysics. Emerson, however, was more hopeful. His method was to make assertions on the basis of intuitive conviction arising from his fundamental nature and then to affirm those intuitive assertions within his experience. Such a risky enterprise meant, of course, that he had to be true to the facts of his experience, no matter what the event or impression. And as we shall see, after 1942 in particular, experience was an exacting teacher. In Emerson's philosophy mind and experience had to be a unity, one and the same. The life consciously lived had to reflect the insights of the mind.

In March of 1840, while staying in Providence, Rhode Island, Emerson made the following observation in his journal:

> When the materialist represents mind as the result of body & at the perishing of the body deceasing—he tells us that this is true, though not so satisfactory to our pride. This last remark is a fatal concession. Nature is always true, there is no lie, no betrayal in it, and yet, it seems in all individuals there arises this feeling on hearing his statement that it is less satisfactory to our pride than something else. In other words, all the individuals feel, here is something wrong, some crack; something else is desirable than that you say is done, something else is best. Then surely something else must be true.[3]

In essays like "The Transcendentalist," this "something else" develops its source as follows:

> The idealist has another measure, which is metaphysical, namely, the "rank" which things themselves take in his consciousness; not

at all, the size or appearance. Mind is the only reality, of which men and all other natures are better or worse reflectors.

In other words, he stands the materialist argument on its head by asserting the ultimate reality of mind only, the body being dead matter perishing. And so, as we look at human nature and see the limitations in each person while we look beyond for the expanse of Universal Mind, Emerson would have us look at nature to understand how the form operates. In "The Method of Nature" Emerson expands upon a journal entry of 1841 (JMN VIII, 19) to make the point.

> The termination of the world in a man, appears to be the last victory of intelligence. The universal does not attract us until housed in an individual. Who heeds the waste abyss of possibility? The ocean is everywhere the same, but it has no character until seen with the shore or the ship. Who would value any number of miles of Atlantic brine bounded by lines of latitude and longitude? Confine it by granite rocks, let it wash a shore where wise men dwell, and it is filled with expression; and the point of greatest interest is where the land and water meet. So must we admire in man, the form of the formless, the concentration of the vast, the house of reason, the cave of memory.

The human being, then, is the point of greatest interest where Mind meets Matter in the vast wastes of the cosmos. The image suggests as well something of the resulting turbulence involved. The image of the "waste abyss of possibility" is striking. The human powers of invention and observation create the point of perception (one sees the captain on his ship, sextant in hand) which brings the abyss within the range of our understanding.

## THE SOURCES OF GENIUS

Emerson's method, like the method of nature, was to place himself in the stream of creative power and there partake of the emanations that flow out of the deepest recesses of the sublime. In his journal for May, 1841, he reported the contents of a dream (or so he called the experience) from which he would draw much of the power for his essay "The Method of Nature."

I walked in my dream with a pundit who said . . . the mind is a stream of thoughts, so was the universe the emanation of God. Every thing is an emanation, & from every emanation is a new emanation, & that from which it emanates is an emanation also. If anything could stand still, it would be instantly crushed & dissipated by the torrent which it resisted, & if it were a mind, would be crazed; as insane persons are those who hold fast to one thought & do not as the mind does, limit & correct it by other thoughts, & so flow with the course of nature.

In order to flow with the course of nature, we place ourselves in the path of this emanation and "limit & correct" with the powers of eloquence and language the flow as it presents itself to our minds. The journal entry (recorded some time in May, 1841) was then revised for a lecture to be delivered at Waterville College in Waterville, Maine, in late summer. In it, Emerson develops this theme and reshapes the image of emanation to meet the secular need, eliminating the dream and the pundit from the account.

The method of nature: who could ever analyze it? That rushing stream will not stop to be observed. We can never surprise nature in a corner; never find the end of a thread; never tell where to set the first stone. The bird hastens to lay her egg: the egg hastens to be a bird. The wholeness we admire in the order of the world, is the result of infinite distribution. Its smoothness is the smoothness of the pitch of the cataract. Its permanence is a perpetual inchoation. Every natural fact is an emanation, and that from which it emanates is an emanation also, and from every emanation is a new emanation. If anything could stand still, it would be crushed and dissipated by the torrent it resisted, and if it were a mind, would be crazed; as insane persons are those who hold fast to one thought, and do not flow with the course of nature. Not the cause, but an ever novel effect, nature descends always from above. It is unbroken obedience. The beauty of these fair objects is imported into them from a metaphysical and eternal spring. In all animal and vegetable forms, the physiologist concedes that no chemistry, no mechanics, can account for the facts, but a mysterious principle of life must be assumed, which not only inhabits the organ, but makes the organ.

Our limits as human beings are often expressed in an inability to circulate with the flowing power of nature. If, as Emerson suggests, insanity resides in holding desperately to one thought, against nature's circulations, then we find our true intellectual and creative health in the ecstasy of intellectual and emotional movement with its flow of emanations in each moment. Emerson claimed that for him this health could find its proper expression only occasionally and usually not in the formalities of lectures and essays whose very composition was balked at every turn by the pressure of deadlines. "The Method of Nature," for example, was deemed a failure when it was delivered, seeming vague in its multiple images of inspiration, which could not have permitted a listener to comprehend the whole. Even in silence of reflective reading, it is a dizzying display.

> In short, the spirit and peculiarity of that impression nature makes on us, is this, that it does not exist to any one or to any number of particular ends, but to numberless and endless benefit; that there is in it no private will, no rebel leaf or limb, but the whole is oppressed by one superincumbent tendency, obeys that redundancy or excess of life which in conscious beings we call "ecstasy."

When Emerson spoke of the need to "let out all the reins," it was in relation to becoming one with the emanations of nature. Giving the horse of nature its head in our heads, as it were, is as crucial to success here as it is seemingly dangerous. The culture of the twentieth century was restrained by Freud's image of the destructive power of the *id* as a runaway horse, with the frightened *ego* sitting astride trying to maintain control over the slippery roads of the *superego*. Whole psychoanalytic systems were built on that image. For Emerson, on the other hand, the laws of the mind, properly seen and understood, coincide with the ecstatic powers of nature's emanations. These are not dark and destructive forces. Our task is to find the freedom to let go of the demands of the individual ego and become one with such power. It was such a message that must have attracted Nietzsche's interest in

Emerson and been at least part of the inspiration for "The Birth of Tragedy," to this day one of the great Neo-Emersonian visions of human creative genius.

In the same month that Emerson recorded his visionary walk with the pundit, he wrote a letter to Margaret Fuller, who in her own genius and aggressive intellectualism had contributed to the opening of the gates of Emerson's uninhibited eloquence. In his letter, which has a feeling of a refreshing break from the limitations of domestic life, Emerson expresses what it would be like to let out all the reins, even for a brief time.

> . . . We could afford then to try experiments & obey all beautiful motions. We could live alone & *if that did not serve,* we could associate. We could enjoy *and* abstain, *and* read *and* burn our books *and* labor *and* dream. But fie on this Half, this Untied, this take-it-or-leave-it, this flash-of-lightning life. In my next migration, O Indra! I bespeak an ampler circle, the "vast year of Mizar & Alcor," an orb, a whole! Come, o my friend, with your earliest convenience, I pray you, & let us seize the void betwixt two atoms of air the vacation between two moments of time to decide how we will steer on this torrent which is called Today.[4]

The use of "torrent" recalls the trope Emerson used above in his lecture—"the smoothness of the pitch of the cataract"—to describe the emanations into which we are to throw ourselves. The sense of danger in "cataract" is a characteristic of Emerson's understanding of the forces involved and the severe limitations imposed by our own inhibitions. It is no wonder that genius, the *daemon* of the Neoplatonists, is so rarely perceived much less followed and that so few of our capabilities find their way into expression. It is not capacity that it limited. It is courage. Or, perhaps it is a capacity for courage.

## PLOTINUS AND THE DAEMON

Emerson's interest in and devotion to the Neoplatonists is well known. He knew Plato, Plotinus, Proclus, and Iamblichus (his life of Pythagoras) through the translations of Thomas Taylor. Essentially a self-taught classicist and therefore suspect among the Oxford and Cambridge scholars of his day,[5] Taylor was a genius and came to his work as a translator with extraordinary intuitive powers. Taylor was an independent scholar, supported by sympathetic patrons, and was acquainted with the leading lights of London during a period of intense interest in all things spiritual and transcendent. He knew William Blake, the sculptor John Flaxman, and other independent intellectuals of the time. He died in 1835, two years after Emerson's first visit to England. Unfortunately, Emerson and Taylor never met.

A brief passage from Taylor's introduction to Plotinus will indicate his mystical tendencies.

> He [Plotinus] was a being wise without the usual mixture of human darkness, and great without the general combination of human weakness and imperfection. He seems to have left *the orb of light* solely for the benefit of mankind; that he might teach them how to repair the ruin contracted by their exile from good, and how to return to their true country, and legitimate kindred and allies.[6]

Taylor is using here the imagery of the bodhisattva of Eastern tradition, the enlightened One who declines Nirvana, or the absorption into the nature of the Absolute, in order to return and teach humankind the Way.[7]

In the context of this chapter and our discussion of genius, Plotinus is crucial. In Emerson's personal copy of the Taylor edition of Plotinus, he marked several passages concerning the *daemon* or genius within each individual. According to Plotinus, each individual possesses a portion of the World-Soul, or Greater *Daemon,* if you will, and this portion actually "presides" over the soul. As such it is, therefore, not identical to the soul in each. In effect, "we obtain a God for the inspective guardian and leader of the soul."[8] Emerson also marked a sentence which clarifies the extent of the guardianship of this *daemon.* "There is one *daemon* who is the guardian and governor of every thing that is in us."[9]

This formulation is employed by Emerson again and again. Not only is there one mind for all, but we are part and parcel of God, who is that mind. The term "genius" always includes this Plotinian sense. In addition, Plotinus brings the three concepts of soul, intellect, and *daemon* into close relation at every turn. The emanation of intellect from World-Soul infuses itself into the human condition to greater or lesser degrees according to the destiny of each. Those abundantly endowed have an innate capacity for spiritual insight. This last hierarchal definition is always part of the Neoplatonic vision, a distinction Emerson accepts as part of the natural order.

The Epilogue of this study has more about the "Dance" of Plotinus and its influence on Emerson's understanding. In this context, however, Plotinus contributes to the image of the individual genius as having its source in Emerson's Oversoul. The image that suggests itself, then, is of a source of power, like a stream of light, within which human beings have their life. We are in it; it is not in us. In this definition, the life of the mind, including the formation of the intellect around its *daemon*, constitutes Reality. The aim of the "work" is to minimize the limitations imposed by circumstances and temperament and to maximize the development of the infinite capacity of mind.

### INTERVAL

Any serious reading of Emerson's thought must give attention to the impact of the death of his first child, Waldo, Jr., on January 27, 1842, at age five. So sudden was his passing that Emerson noted that the Sunday before he had carried Waldo to church to see the new organ and the next Sunday carried the body to church for the funeral. The cause was scarlet fever. The boy was stricken on Monday and although everyone was aware of the dangers, Waldo's death on Thursday was a tremendous shock.

The following entries in Journal J for the next several weeks of 1842 speak volumes:

28 JAN

Yesterday night at 15 minutes after eight my little Waldo ended his life.

30 JAN

What he looked upon is better, what he looked not upon is

insignificant. The morning of Friday I woke at 3 o'clock, & every cock in every barnyard was shrilling with the most unnecessary noise. The sun went up the morning sky with all his light, but the landscape was dishonored by this loss. For this boy in whose remembrance I have both slept & wakened so oft, decorated for me the morning star, & the evening cloud,—how much more all the particulars of daily economy; for he had touched with his lively curiosity every trivial fact & circumstance in the household—the hard coal & the soft coal which I put into my stove; the wood of which he brought his little quota for grandmother's fire, the hammer, the pincers, & file, he was so eager to use; the microscope, the magnet, the little globe, & every trinket & instrument in the study; the loads of gravel on the meadow, the nests in the henhouse and many & many a little visit to the doghouse & barn,—For every thing he had his own name & way of thinking, his own pronunciation & manner. And every word came mended from that tongue. A boy of early wisdom, of a grave & even majestic deportment, of a perfect gentleness.

He gave up his innocent breath like a bird.

Sorrow makes us all children again, destroys all differences of intellect. The wisest knows nothing.

Waldo asked if the strings of the harp open when he touches them.[10]

This loss was both inexplicable and incomprehensible. The death of his first wife Ellen ten years before, though deeply felt by the young Emerson so much in love, was anticipated if not expected. He had watched her weaken and had fully understood the dangers of her wasting condition. Young Waldo, on the other hand, although not a robust child, was nonetheless healthy and active until the last.

In reaction to the death, Emerson wrote to Margaret Fuller to say that he doubted he would ever dare to love again. He did not, however, lapse into traditional rationalizations. Although his wife and mother wrote in their letters the traditional Christian pieties for the early death of innocents, Emerson's only similar declaration was made in a letter to Caroline Sturgis, a close friend to both Emerson and Fuller: "Dear Boy too precious & unique a creation to be huddled aside into the waste & prodigality of things,"[11] It was as if, at least in this special case, here was a human being not made for the turbulence of nature.

Soon after, Emerson had to travel to Providence to begin a series of lectures. He wrote often to his wife Lidian, knowing that she was grieving deeply and was not able to function normally. Even though two remaining children, Ellen and Edith, needed her constant attention, she would take months to recover some semblance of normal life and years to overcome her grief. Writing from Providence on February 15, Emerson noted with sadness that after a week there he had not received a letter from her.

> Much I fear, dear Wife, that the Post Office has bro't me no letter this day, for it is 1 o'clock, & Mr. Fuller would have sent me one, had he found it. And so for a whole week you have written me no syllable of the poor children, for whom I suppose you think I do not care, nor of yourself nor of Mother. Well, is this to punish my philosophy?[12]

The differences between husband and wife in matters of faith, such as the existence of a personal God or the solaces of heaven, emerge here, somewhat defensively, in this crisis. Emerson would not slide into comforting myth for the sake of Lidian, no more than he would shake his fist at heaven in anger or despair. He would drive his grief into a corner, trap it, and eventually transform it. Two years later, in his crucial essay "Experience," Emerson would place the event in philosophical context:

> Grief too will make us idealists. In the death of my son, now more than two years ago, I seem to have lost a beautiful estate,—no more. I cannot get it nearer to me. If tomorrow I should be informed of the bankruptcy of my principal debtors, the loss of my property would be a great inconvenience to me, perhaps, for many years; but it would leave me as it found me,—neither better nor worse. So is it with this calamity: it does not touch me: some thing which I fancied was a part of me, which could not be torn

away without tearing me, nor enlarged without enriching me, falls off from me, and leaves no scar. It was caducous. I grieve that grief can teach me nothing, nor carry me one step into real nature.

Even though Emerson characterizes the death of little Waldo as the seasonal dropping of leaves, leaving us momentarily saddened as another summer and brilliant fall come to an end, we find it hard to fit this image into the reality of the loss. When in the crisis of his own death, on April 27, 1882, Emerson murmured "Oh, that beautiful boy!" it is assumed that he was speaking of Waldo, whose image must have come to him in the crisis. What he says in "Experience," however, teaches us how to confront loss and go on, as go on we must. The loss of my own daughter while deeply engaged in the study of Emerson taught me as much.

Commentators have duly noted the change in Emerson's tone and imagery after 1842, and certainly the death of Waldo both marks and causes a change. Steven Whicher's seminal *Freedom and Fate* (1953) made the case of fundamental change in this period, asserting a falling away of Emerson's essential optimism and idealism. Although some hold to this view, there is another: Emerson's vision, reflected powerfully in the magnificent essay "Circles," is a continuous drawing of the huge arc of a philosophy that radiates out from the core of the book *Nature* and becomes more and more grounded in the conduct of life rather than more general. This process of radiating out from a central vision into specificity naturally entails attention to the more banal and brutal facts of daily existence. As we are all worn down by circumstance, so are we supported by deeply held conviction at the core, which in its essence may never be rejected even as it is smoothed down by the passage of turbulent events.

The death of Waldo did indeed mark a severe testing of Emerson's idealism. His comment to Margaret Fuller that he might never dare to love again could have been a severe blow to his philosophy and a clouding of his vision. In Idealism, the heart must be open to life, to its people and its events. Closing down leaves the intellect cold, opening the mind to sarcasm and eventually to cynicism and bitterness. No evidence of this kind of decline emerges in Emerson's journals or formal work after this period. Indeed the bulk of Emerson's work appears after 1842, and he remained focused and productive for at least twenty more years. That he focused more attention on Fate and Power after 1842 speaks to his broad creative purpose, not to any essential impairment of his vision.

Finally, in a prophetic note, Emerson described a moment he shared with little Waldo and Henry Thoreau, who had been living with the Emersons and who spent as much time with the boy as did his father. Waldo is asking questions.

> "Are there any other countries?" Yes. "I wish you to name the other countries" so I went on to name London, Paris, Amsterdam, Cairo, &c. But HDT well said in allusion to his large way of speech that "his questions did not admit of an answer; they were the same which you would ask yourself."[13]

This "large way of speech" had impressed Thoreau, and stories of Waldo's poetic prodigality had come back to Emerson from friends and visitors to the house. Waldo was curious about other realities. Not only was his first-born lost, but also a far-seeing, prophetic sensibility. And for Emerson, these losses were crucial. When his brother Charles died, Emerson lost a stimulating voice and perceptive eye. And when Margaret Fuller was drowned in the storm off the coast of Long Island in 1850, he lost yet another vital companion of the spirit. Despite these losses, however, the progression of the soul in matter, as Emerson called the examined life, continued.

# *10*    PROGRESS OF THE SOUL

*Once awakened* to the life of the mind, the seeker wishes to maintain a certain progress. Unlike the discovery of a fixed piece of actual territory, the opening of the life of the mind creates a vast sense of space that asks to be filled. The philosopher enters this newly opened space to seek greater insight.

Emerson saw himself and other idealists as making a transformational progress through matter. The physical body was, as Emerson saw it, the study or office where he did his work. As such it was limited and confined, as opposed to the mind, which offers limitless expanse and opportunity. As Emerson saw it, if the best we can say of God is "the mind as it is made known to us," our God-seeking and soul-awakening progress is made through knowledge of the workings of the human mind—and this necessarily means awakening to Mind in its largest cosmic sense. That this work is transformational means that any change is permanent and substantive.

At this stage in Emerson's journey, the late 1840s, the progress was not so much God-seeking in the sense of personifications of Deity. It was more a deeper understanding of incarnation, bringing the attributes of God through the Mind into the experience of human life, and there transforming the whole life into a more sublime articulation of the divine presence. Such an ambition was bound to bring with it failure and disappointment, and the journals reflect that tone often. As already noted, observers have suggested as a result that after 1842 Emerson fell away from his idealism. What is much more likely is that he became more sanguine about the nature of progress itself. His experiment, after all, was a momentous one, especially since it was

*Emerson in lecture garb, 1842*

being carried out in the conduct of his life and not merely in philosophical speculations.

Emerson conducted the work of knowing the mind, its faculties and operations, through two practices: reflection and observation. The focus of his observations was, as always, nature and its hidden laws. He knew that if he could live his life and maintain his thought in sympathy with the Universal Laws of Nature, he would come as close as possible to incarnating God in and through his being. Knowing full well that his physical body operated on the level of biological laws, he maintained throughout his life an interest in scientific progress. His reading habits in various fields, although never reaching a majority of his interest by any means, always included the latest scientific thinking.[1] He wished to know the limitations as well as the possibilities. He never regarded science as an enemy of idealism.

The progress of mind/brain research in the twentieth century has narrowed the abyss once separating these terms. Yet we still—despite recent materialist assertions coming out of Cambridge, England, in particular—cannot say that all the functions and faculties of mind are found in the electrochemical operations of the brain and nervous system. Mind is a term only recently being allowed back into the discussion. The current fashion is that it is the culmination of evolutionary development and philosophical thinking incorporating cursive thinking, reasoning, and various levels of consciousness. Despite the attempt by the field of psychology in the early to mid-twentieth century to eliminate the word "mind" from its deliberations, the term is back because it is needed to describe subtle levels of human mental activity so far unclaimed by brain activity, but now expanded to the entire cellular mechanism. Everywhere we look, the science of mind is an active, vital discipline, enhanced these days by a willingness of biologists and philosophers to open a dialogue once again to questions of consciousness. Agreement is lacking, but the dialogue has once again begun.

Also, the transformation of silicon chips into the abyss of cyberspace gives fresh support to both materialists and idealists. The former see computer technology as analogous to the mind/brain, type/type identity, whereas the latter see such transformation as evidence of the mind's transformation of matter through subtle energies.

Emerson would certainly have been in the forefront of such discussions, as William James was a generation later. His intense interest in the fundamental laws of science led him to articulate the correspondences between physiological attribute and mental perception and functioning. In his view, human beings are receivers of subtle impulses which the organism translates into images and then into language. His view would be that modern researchers ignore the impulses in favor of narrow mechanistic concerns. We are conduits, not originators.

Here is Emerson's position on the issue. The Mind and the Soul are part of the great law of the cosmos and are both universal in aspect and function. The Great Consciousness, or Over-Soul, pervades matter, animating it with life and infusing it with the potential for personal transformation. The human being is the best transformational organ on the planet, having about it potential articulation. Genius is the evidence of such potential in vivid operation. Limitation consists in an unwillingness to perceive or an inability to awaken sufficiently to progress. Endowment in this arena is ubiquitous but unequal.

If this relation of levels of consciousness between the divine and human is an accurate description, there needs to be a new description of what constitutes good and evil, at least in historical terms. In other words, we can no longer "blame" a distinctly personal God for failing to intervene in human affairs. Nor can we attribute every apparently human action to something called human nature as defined separately from God's. The highest universal laws are operations of an intelligence emanating from God. Human beings are capable, through the awakening of a higher capacity of understanding, of grasping these laws and applying them to human life. What constitutes inhumanity and evil is the result of human failure to partake of these higher laws. As such, the responsibility for that failure is completely our own.

History, as a reflection of this activity, is the biography of human progress. It is the account of the human soul's progress in matter written on a global scale. As such human beings are *always* culpable for acts of inhumanity. Had he witnessed the atrocities of the twentieth century, Emerson would have explained the Holocaust, or any genocide, as human in origin and originating from insufficient force on the part of more enlightened, conscious human beings to prevent such evil from occurring. Some have seen this analysis as the failure of a weak God, that is of a deity too distant or incapacitated by the force of evil to counteract its tendencies. This frustration with the apparent weakness of the forces of good ignores the nature of what good as a force looks like and how it operates. Evil as the negation of good is always more dramatic in its effects. Tragedy is always more memorable than comedy.

In 1844, Emerson penned "Experience," his challenging examination of evil and "the dark side" of human life. In it he faced questions that were set aside or undeveloped in the earlier essays and lectures, in which his essential idealism set the tone for his life's work. Indeed throughout this next decade, roughly between 1844 and 1854, he would spiral out to the questions of experience, wealth, and power and would have to answer critics who said that he was attending too much to the devil's work. One answer to that criticism was made in "Experience."

> Saints are sad, because they behold sin, (even when they specu-late,) from the point of view of the conscience, and not of the intellect; a confusion of thought. Sin seen from the thought, is a diminution or "less": seen from the conscience or will, it is pravi-ty or "bad". The intellect names it shade, absence of light, and no essence. The conscience must feel it as essence, essential evil. This it is not: it has an objective existence, but no subjective.

This distinction between the intellect and conscience is important. In Emerson's lexicon "conscience" is a feeling that takes hold of the human instrument in moments of depravity to say "No." It is a social guide, innate but culturally tutored. On the other hand, intellect is that innate capacity of mind which perceives higher relations and is not touched by feeling. The intellect sees evil as the absence of good, as darkness is the absence of light and not a force that blocks light. Seen as privation, evil can also be linked to the symbol of a sleeping soul, to a state of ignorance unchecked by the light of the intellect penetrating the darkness.

Therefore, if the soul is to progress in matter, the mind has to be ruled by the seeing intellect and to master feelings that can so easily overwhelm it. This mastery by the intellect was characterized by Emer-son as self-poise. It is the detachment that is characteristic of the philosophical stance, the detached acceptance of loss and the objective, non-egoistic regard of success. One measure of progress is this rigor-ous detachment from life's blows.

If some perceive of this detachment as an unfeeling lack of compassion for the condition of the less fortunate, Emerson was ready to accept that criticism. He said in several places, most famously in "Self-Reliance," that charity based merely on sentimental feeling is false giving. Either principle rules one's giving or the gift is seriously misplaced. In other words,

> Your goodness must have some edge to it,—else it is none. The doctrine of hatred must be preached as the counteraction of the doctrine of love when that pules and whines. I shun father and mother and wife and brother, when my genius calls me. I would write on the lintels of the door-post, "Whim." I hope it is somewhat better than whim at last, but we cannot spend the day in explanation. Expect me not to show cause why I seek or why I exclude company. Then, again, do not tell me, as a good man did to-day, of my obligation to put all poor men in good situations. Are they *my* poor? I tell thee, thou foolish philanthropist, that I grudge the dollar, the dime, the cent, I give to such men as do not belong to me and to whom I do not belong. There is a class of persons to whom by all spiritual affinity I am bought and sold; for them I will go to prison, if need be; but your miscellaneous popular charities; the education at college of fools; the building of meeting-houses to the vain end to which many now stand; alms to sots; and the thousandfold Relief Societies;—though I confess with shame I sometimes succumb and give the dollar, it is a wicked dollar which by and by I shall have the manhood to withhold.

Seen by some as Emerson's essential lack of liberal or Christian compassion, what we are really witnessing is the rule of the intellect and the primacy of principle in the soul's progress in matter. Emerson's devotion to those who were in spiritual prisons, whom if he did not visit no one would, establishes his spiritual priorities. What we are seeing here is the power of discrimination at work and the absence of sentimentalism in judgment. He was embodying Plato's dictum that true justice is knowing your work and not doing the work of others.

To some extent, this protective coloring was essential to Emerson's idealism. If sentimentalism were to creep into his philosophy, the foundation would quickly crumble. We see this fact daily in the excesses of the so-called New Age movement, where intellect is not given a high priority. Emerson's idealism was elitist in the sense of separating those who fight to stay awake from those who habitually sleep. When the intellect is awake, the self-poise that results provides a discriminating judgment that surface conditions can not penetrate. His serious seekers formed a natural aristocracy of the spirit, a designation which Emerson placed firmly against aristocracy by class or economic status.

A proper reading of "Self-Reliance" reveals the demanding standards by which this aristocracy must make its proper progress in matter. Society does not and will not help. In fact, the social matrix that arises around the individual inhibits rather than stimulates genuine spiritual progress. When Emerson resigned his post as a minister, he ceased to present himself in a social framework easily defined by traditional social standards. Quite consciously he created his professional and personal identity each day and each year, sometimes lecturing, sometimes attending meetings, and sometimes accepting assignments like the editorship of *The Dial* (a task he felt took him away from his real work). Indeed, his detachment from pursuing a profession and maintaining social position made it necessary for him to establish firm standards of outside participation. And even then, because his house stood along the Cambridge Turnpike, his door was frequently opened to unannounced visitors. His patience with such interruption was legendary.

As the passage above from "Self-Reliance" indicates, genius (or the presence of the awakened soul in matter) requires a different and higher standard when its actions are manifest in the world. The chance for misunderstanding is obvious. Emerson's sensitivity to that fact shaped his conduct of life and the second half of his career as a public writer and lecturer. That he seemed to write "down" to a broader audience after 1845 reflects his growing role as America's Seer. He felt a deep personal responsibility to serve those who asked him to lecture and publish his views. His private investigations, however, continued unabated at a high level of philosophical inquiry. Their focus was maintained very privately among the inner circle of friends and correspondents with whom he maintained a nearly continuous dialogue.

## THE INNER CIRCLE

In "Circles," Emerson took his philosophical compass and inscribed an arc describing the laws by which he lived. That arc, which was always partial and expanding, attracted like minds to his center. As the circumference of his personal influence expanded to national dimensions, he scrupulously maintained a tight circle of friends and correspondents who shared his vision. In "Circles," he described the nature of the relationship:

> The life of man is a self-evolving circle, which, from a ring imperceptibly small, rushes on all sides outwards to new and larger circles, and that without end. The extent to which this generation of circles, wheel without wheel, will go, depends on the force or truth of the individual soul.

Central to maintaining the "force or truth" of the individual soul is the discipline of self-observation, keeping an eye on one's personal outward actions and inner life. If confession is good for the soul, even more critical is observation; and Emerson's inner circle watched one another with care and love.

The collected letters of Emerson and his friends reveal this special purpose. The central figures were four women and four men, at least as revealed in their correspondence. The local friends in Concord—Thoreau, Alcott, and to some extent Hawthorne—were never consistent correspondents. Their relationship to Emerson took the form of walking partners; the only records of the nature of their conversations appear occasionally in Emerson's journals. The women in Emerson's circle, on the other hand, were the most important in this special role of reflective observation. Margaret Fuller, Caroline Sturgis, Elizabeth Hoar, and, to some extent Lidian Emerson (My Asia) all served in this capacity. The men were Thomas Carlyle, Charles King Newcome, Samuel Gray Ward, and Frederick Henry Hedge. They were not always compatible in their philosophical orientation, especially Carlyle and Hedge, but they nonetheless served this special purpose. It was the women, however, who served Emerson's own personal journey so well with their special gifts of inner sight.

In our own time, the close relationship with correspondents is lost on us, letter writing being such a lost art. It is difficult even to fathom the extent of the correspondence Emerson maintained. His letters, not all complete, constitute at present six volumes. With no telephone or tele-anything, the time spent in hotel rooms over the years provided ample opportunity to keep up with the lives of his friends. Even in Concord, some time was set aside on a regular basis for letter writing. Emerson understood the way in which friends of like mind can stimulate one another to expansive visions and also provide needed moments of personal reflection. From "Friends":

> Our intellectual and active powers increase with our affection. The scholar sits down to write, and all his years of meditation do not furnish him with one good thought or happy expression; but it is necessary to write a letter to a friend,—and, forthwith, troops of gentle thoughts invest themselves, on every hand, with chosen words.

The special relationship of friends to the inner work of the progress of the soul in matter was crucial to Emerson. Although he wished to proceed without teachers, relying on his own inner resources, there was a need for checks and balances. It was almost as if the arrival of like-minded spirits came to him as a welcome surprise, so much the loner had he been in the formative years. Again from "Friends":

> My friends have come to me unsought. The great God gave them to me. By oldest right, by the divine affinity of virtue with itself, I find them, or rather not I, but the Deity in me and in them derides and cancels the thick walls of individual character, relation, age, sex, circumstance, at which he usually connives, and now makes many one. High thanks I owe you, excellent lovers, who carry out the world for me to new and noble depths, and enlarge the meaning of all my thoughts.

What was important about these friends was their dedication to important issues, to "noble depths." Most important, his friends refrained as much as possible from empty gossip, that deadly game of "Did you know that . . . " which reduces us to voyeurs in the superficial matters of daily life. In towns like Concord, the provincial attitudes of neighbors living in close proximity make gossip the normal pattern of social activity. Emerson's decision to live in Concord in the first place was made primarily on the basis of its potential peace and quiet, relief from the noise and distractions of city life. But the provincialism of small town life was also a challenge. Emerson managed to take part in the life of the town and still avoid most of the evils of living in the proverbial fishbowl, especially as he become more famous. He observed, for example, that when he entered a store, normal conversation ceased, almost as if his presence brought the gossipers to heel.

Emerson was obviously privy to all sorts of intimate knowledge of people in his personal and community circles. It is a testament to his character that he did not stoop to gossip, especially given the extent of his journal and letter writing. What is clear, however, from the extensive record of people's lives contained in these pages is Emerson's primary focus upon ideas and significant thought, in other words, the life of the mind. He was intensely interested in character, and it was often the talk of the inner circle.

The kind of self-observation and reflective watching we are speaking of in relation to Emerson's inner circle was not of the self-conscious variety. That is, there was never any overt discussion of this activity as an agreed-upon spiritual discipline, as we might find in a religious community such as at Brook Farm—that experiment in communal spirituality of which Emerson was an interested party but not a participant. As we shall see, the kind of self-knowledge that emerged in these communications was an effect of the deep concern and mutual affection these friends shared. Theirs was a philosophy based on spiritual progress. Looking inward was part of the effort to improve their days.

We begin our look at this special correspondence with a letter from Emerson to Margaret Fuller. It was written from New York City in March, 1842, just two months after the death of young Waldo Emerson. It was a time of special care in the communication between these two close friends.

Margaret was seven years Emerson's junior and had by 1842 (at age thirty-two) established herself as an intellectual presence in New

England. She was extraordinarily gifted and would eventually make her reputation as the author of *Women in the Nineteenth Century*, regarded as one of the first and foremost feminist documents written in America. Shortly after this period of close correspondence with Emerson, she emigrated to Europe, eventually to settle in Italy, have a son, and then marry his father, the Count Ossoli. She would end her life at sea in 1850 by drowning off the shores of Fire Island as the ship "Elizabeth" was battered to bits in a hurricane. It was another pivotal loss to Emerson from the inner circle.

In this 1842 letter Emerson takes a wry look at the people he has met in New York and reflects on the unique atmosphere that both repelled and attracted him during his stay.

> . . . Yesterday I dined with Horace Greely [sic] and with Brisbane the socialist at their Graham boarding house. Greely is a young man with white soft hair from New Hampshire, mother of men, of sanguine temper & liberal mind, no scholar but such a one as journals & newspapers make, who listens after all new thoughts & things but with the indispensable New York condition that they be made available; likes the thought but must keep the power; What can I do with such an abettor? He declares himself a Transcendentalist, is a unitarian, a defender of miracles, &c. I saw my fate in a moment & that I should never content him. Brisbane wished to know how the "Trans." &c established the immortality of the soul. He had never believed in it until he learned it of Fourier, who completely established it! Alas, how shall I content Mr. Brisbane?
> . . . these kindly but too determinate persons, the air of Wall Street, the expression of the faces of the male & female crown in Broadway, the endless rustle of newspapers all make me feel not the value of their classes but of my own class—the supreme need of the few worshippers of the Muse—wild & sacred—as counteraction to this world of material & ephemeral interest. Lidian sometimes taxes me at home with an egotism more virulent than any against which I rail. Perhaps she is right.[2]

That last comment arose from Emerson's refusal in that context to discuss the fine points of his "wild and sacred" philosophy. It was not his place or habit to focus attention on the beliefs of others. What he had recognized was the tendency of Greely and Brisbane to juggle what Emerson saw as a "material and ephemeral" duality in their thinking. How could he satisfy both sides of their philosophy at once?

The letter also mentions Eclecticism, then popular as an influence among intellectuals in New York. It was the movement coming from France in the thinking of Victor Cousin (1792–1867). The emphasis here was certainly parallel to Transcendentalism with its careful observation of the life consciously lived, but the emphasis was on a metaphysical gathering of a variety of philosophic ideas and systems, which was certainly contrary to Emerson's views. As he said in the letter, "I must unfold my own thought." In Boston, everyone stood firm in his or her belief; but in New York, Emerson found an open forum of ideas and a kind of shopping for a place to stand. He saw himself suddenly as a salesman.

His letter concludes with an interesting bit of self-awareness, perhaps prompted by the overwhelming sense of power and energy he felt in New York, which as a city was growing as no other place on the continent was growing, even in the face of depressed economic conditions elsewhere.

> Pity me & comfort me, O my friend, in this city of magnificence & of steam. For a national, for an imperial prosperity, everything here seems irrevocably destined. What a Bay! What a River! what climate! what men! What ample interior domain, lake, mountain & forest! What manners, what histories & poetry shall rapidly arise & for how long, and it seems, endless date! Me my cabin fits better, yet very likely from a certain poorness of spirit; but in my next transmigration, I think I should choose New York.[3]

His wry comment about reincarnation did not relate to any specific belief on his part (other than a profound respect for his Eastern influences), but it points instead to the limits of his own constitution in this lifetime. "My cabin" points both to Concord and to his lack of physical hardiness—the cramped office/body where he worked—and to "a certain poorness of spirit."

This last image echoed a theme that haunted Emerson throughout his life. He felt that previous generations had squandered much of his ancestral genetic fire, as it were, and had sent him into the world "scarce half made up," to paraphrase Shakespeare's Richard. That he did live to be seventy-nine does not altogether prove this concern to be exaggerated, because he felt always that he suffered from limited reserves of energy on a day-to-day basis in the effort to accomplish the goals he set for himself. The loss of Waldo at age five and the consistent frailty of his second son Edward seemed further proof of his point.

To counteract this perception of dampened fires, Emerson encouraged in his correspondence an open passion of thought, if not of physical expression. Margaret's communications to Emerson possessed the character of intense and passionate openness. On March 8, 1842, she wrote:

> Dearest Waldo;
>
> My letter comes along tardily, but I have been ill much of the time, and the better days so full of the enforced indolence of the bad days that thoughts and feelings have had no chance to grow for the absent. Yet that is not all, there has been a sort of incubus on me when I looked your way, it disappears when we meet, but it returns to prevent my writing. Your letter drives it away from the present. I have thought of you many times, indeed in all my walks, and in the night, with unspeakable tenderness, in the same way I see you in the letter and of that time when you were in N. York, two years ago, so much that I have been trying to go to Cambridge and get your letter in which after seeing the ships go by, you turn to the little dead flowers of the year before that grew upon the wall—But I suppose you have forgotten all about it,—I will not follow this path; . . .[4]

The obvious affection and longing attached to this letter are part and parcel of the relationships in the inner circle, a condition Emerson handled with great care, but also supported because it meant vitality and honesty. In his response to Margaret, who concluded her letter with the plea, "Tell me more about those dim New Yorkers," he told her of a certain Mrs. Black, a spiritual woman whom he dismissed for being "serene and self sufficing." He went on to describe others he had met.

> I have seen Miss Sedgewick, & Bryant, but I believe I have nothing to tell you of them. Bryant is greatly interested in homeopathy and is himself an active practitioner. The cold man gets warm in telling his stories of his cures. He is always to me a pleasing person so clean & unexceptionable in his manners, so full of facts, and quiet as a good child, but Miss Sedgewick complained of his coldness, she had known him always & and never saw him warm. I have become acquainted with a very intelligent person named Henry James . . . and his brother John, who read very good books; and the former, at least, is an independent right minded man.[5]

The relationship to the James family would become one of the most important in Emerson's life. In his first visit to the James' home in New York, he blessed the young sleeping William James, aged one.

Later that fall, Margaret wrote again to articulate something of her emotional struggle with her relationship to Emerson, which was very complex. She told him, "I get, after a while, even *intoxicated* with your mind, and do not live enough in myself."[6] Her efforts in correspondence were to clarify the thoughts which were solely hers in contrast to those which were his, a problem shared as well by Thoreau in his intimacy with Emerson. To Margaret, Emerson replied,

> Thanks again for your coming to see me, & for your kindly behaviour to the old & incapable churl. But I will not go on with the details of my gratitude, for why should I thank you for existing. Undoubtedly you find your own account in that and much that is substantial benefit to me is an inevitable fruit.[7]

Here again is the encouragement, the shifting of focus to what is important from what might turn neurotic in their relationship. His self-deprecating humor held the relationship at arm's length while reaffirming his dedication to her and all she meant to him.

It was the fundamental consistency over the years that held the inner circle together, the conviction that the philosophy emerging from Emerson's pen was held in common among these few close friends. They could share the common ground while they kept the rest of the world at bay. A final example may seal the point. In a subsequent trip to New York to give another series of lectures, Emerson wrote Margaret to reaffirm once again the importance of what he called his Proven Friends.

> I have much thrust upon me—Fourierists wish to indoctrinate me & give me "short notes on commerce" of 14 sheets to read. Quakers give me printed pamphlets to read; intelligent separatists wish to read me a few MS. pages that I may "take their idea." Mrs. Black & other saints wish me to come to their "little meeting" just a couple of hours . . .[8]

New York was, as always, a melting pot; but in this case it seemed more of a stew of ideas and systems, all competing for attention. Emerson's reputation by 1843 made him the target of anyone who wished to promote their system and who seemed to need his approval. It would be a benefit to anyone's view of the world to harness Emerson's eloquence on its behalf. Of course, all of them missed the point entirely. Here was Emerson saying, "Think for yourself. Be an endless seeker with no past at your back. Look at the mind in the moment and see what is needed, what arises there." No wonder he was silent in company. And even when he lectured, misunderstanding plagued him. As he told Margaret, "I have sent you no newspapers simply because the report is so ruinous to what truth & proportion is in my stories, that I cannot read them."[9]

Even though Margaret Fuller was only seven years Emerson's junior, she seemed much younger. This was partly because Emerson had been since the early 1830s a figure of prominence and she was only beginning to emerge. As a result, she was concerned with action, while Emerson was content with his more limited role, which saw action as interruption. Fuller's contribution to Emerson's work, similar to Thoreau's contribution, may well be seen as a spur keeping him in the fray. She reminded him of his obligation to speak out on social issues, particularly slavery, the central issue of American life as the 1850s loomed. Thus, Emerson's search for divinity began to focus on human action and its relation to fundamental justice.

# *11* THE WORLD COMES AROUND

*As the decade* of the 1850s began, the politics of slavery began more and more to occupy the country. The Fugitive Slave Law, originally passed in 1793 and designed to ensure that escaped slaves would be apprehended and returned to their owners, had never been much enforced in the North. Now, with Daniel Webster's influence (through his eloquence) and the support of a merchant Boston tied to Southern economic interests, the law was being enforced in Massachusetts for the first time. Slavery became a personal matter for Emerson. He was touched by the law as never before. Escaped slaves, who had been going through Concord on their way north to Canada, were at risk for capture. Emerson and his friends stood to be arrested for aiding them.

The issue came to a head in April, 1851. An escaped slave, Thomas Sims, was ordered to be returned to Georgia from prison in Boston, where he had been held awaiting a ship for passage. Last minute attempts to gain Sims' release failed. Emerson wrote in his journal, speaking of the Fugitive Slave Law: ". . . this filthy enactment was made in the 19th Century by people who could read & write. I will not obey it, by God!"[1] His refusal would not be passive. Here was principle touching him, and despite his great hesitation in participating in political matters, he became, after 1851, one of the country's most effective Abolitionists.

The importance of this issue to our immediate interest is its application of spiritual principles to the active life, and to the misplaced attention Emerson drew to himself as a result. It was also a transformational issue, affecting fundamental perceptions of the human condition.

Slavery was not Emerson's life's work, yet he came to the issue from the position of one who had observed how individuals and institutions ignored the moral law in defending it. First, there was the failure of Christianity as an institution to respond to slavery. Second, there was the moral failure of the writers of the Constitution to respond. Thomas Jefferson's inability to force inclusion of any reference to slavery in the documents of the republic, plus his own ownership of more than a hundred slaves through most of his life, exposed the moral weakness of American institutions in the face of economic self-interest and racial bigotry. What Emerson stood for in his isolation from such institutions was embodied in principles of freedom and personal integrity. From his first exposure to slavery in Florida many years before, these principles made any form of enforced servitude an abomination. A slave kindly treated was still a slave. It was a matter of idea and conduct, working together.

How far Emerson's position varied from the general attitude in Boston during this period is illustrated by the overt support Webster received for his position that the Fugitive Slave Law should be enforced. In March, 1850, a letter signed by more than nine hundred persons, including many Unitarian ministers, praised Webster in print for all to witness. One signer was Oliver Wendell Holmes, who was later one of Emerson's biographers (and who, incidentally, glosses over the issue of slavery in his appraisal of this period of Emerson's life and work).

Despite his general admiration for Webster, Emerson could not forgive the New Hampshire senator for the fundamental failure in this compromise over slavery. Emerson would have been willing to see the country divide permanently over the issue. As he noted in his journal, "Ask not, is it constitutional? Ask, is it right?"[2] Union was not larger than morality, a fact lost on Webster and most Americans at the time. Here was a true test of the spirit that had founded the country. Was it to be economic freedom only? Was the revolution about taxation? Were we to be a nation "under God"?

Emerson seldom spoke to public questions. His own task—as he saw it and explained in the opening passage of "The Fugitive Slave Law"— was to attend to those who were imprisoned spiritually, whom if he did

*Emerson in his late fifties, at the height of his public fame*

not visit, would never know true freedom. Here, he explained, was such a case. Those who supported slavery or its laws were themselves imprisoned spiritually. Emerson vowed to visit them with his moral force. Freedom in mind and freedom in body were related.

Also, there was the issue of abandonment, particularly of his role as a writer of messages to the spiritually imprisoned. All his work for more than fifteen years had been centered on the theme of self-trust and the progress of the soul in matter. Here now was slavery coming to his door and making its evil presence known to him on a personal basis. Emerson's devotion to experience, to responding only to what touched him personally, made him wait until slavery came to his door.

When eventually it did, he responded forcefully. Webster had personally directed his attention.

When his own actions in support of runaway slaves became illegal and the law imposed itself upon the expression of these actions, he was forced against his personal taste into the public arena. The result was a power and eloquence not found in Emerson's work since the epiphanies of the late 1830s and early 1840s. Warming to his task, he wrote in his journal:

> We shall never feel well again until that detestable law is nullified in Massachusetts & until the Government is assured that once for all it cannot & shall not be executed here. All I have, and all I can do shall be given & done in opposition to the execution of the law.[3]

Emerson's way was not to assume an attitude of moral indignation or express moral superiority as a personal stance. His method was to find exemplars of moral loftiness and offer his eloquence to their glory. His praise of John Brown has that influence, and his funeral oration for Theodore Parker served his immediate purpose even better. In praising Parker, who had died while visiting Florence in 1860, Emerson used the occasion to admonish those who would compromise principle.

> . . . the essence of Christianity is its practical morals; it is there for use, or it is nothing; and if you combine it with sharp trading, or with ordinary city ambitions to gloze over municipal corruptions, or private intemperance, or successful fraud, or immoral politics, or unjust wars, or the cheating of Indians, or the robbery of frontier nations, or leaving your principles at home to follow on the high seas or in Europe a supple complaisance to tyrants,— it is a hypocrisy, and the truth is not in you. . . . His ministry fell on a political crisis also; on the years when the Southern slavery broke over its old banks, made new and vast pretensions, and wrung from the weakness or treachery of Northern people fatal concessions in the fugitive Slave Bill and the repeal of the Missouri Compromise. . . . In terrible earnest [Parker] denounced the public crime, and meted out to every official high and low, his due portion.[4]

Saying "the truth is not in you" places the failure squarely in its philosophical and spiritual context. Truth is either present or not. God is active within or not. The world of opinion (Plato's *doxa*), in which much illusory latitude is granted, is a world of relative values in which each individual may hold whatever views he or she finds convenient. The truth, however, is severe in its demands and is never relative. There must have been those present to honor Parker who reddened at Emerson's truth.

What permitted Emerson this powerful license, this temerity to stand before the mourners of Theodore Parker and call their integrity into question, was the foundation he had established for himself years before and articulated in "Self-Reliance." In it he said,

> They did not yet see, and thousands of young men as hopeful now crowding to the barriers for the career, do not yet see, that, if the single man plant himself indomitably on his instincts, and there abide, the huge world will come round to him.

In the confusion in which America found itself throughout the 1850s, voices like Emerson's were as profoundly needed as they were violently rejected. Personal safety seemed to require compromise and a willingness to accept immorality for the sake of one's family. The merchants of Boston were bound by economic ties to slavocracy. But these conditions always exist. Slavery still exists. In Africa, young girls are sold into slavery to atone for the sins of their parents. Our clothes are still made by slave labor in Asian sweat-shops, and mills close in New England just as they did when war interrupted the easy flow of cheap cotton into Boston harbor.

In a crucial journal entry, from November, 1838, when Emerson was first in the public eye and fighting for his philosophic life, he made an observation about how one judges the work of another.

> The infallible index of the true progress is found in the tone of the man. Neither his age nor his breeding nor company nor books nor actions nor talents, nor all together can hinder him from being deferential to a higher spirit than his own. If he have not found his home in God, his manners, his forms of speech, the construc-

tion of his sentences, the build of his opinions will involuntarily confess it, let him brave it out how he will. If he have found his centre, the commanding God will shine through him, through all the disguises of modesty, of ignorance, of ungenial temperament. The tone of seeking is one, & the tone of having is another.[5]

This entry finds itself here, in the argument over slavery, because Emerson's loss of respect for Webster was really disappointment in his loss of the man's center and in the tone, as well as the substance, of speeches and declarations Webster was making in these days. The infamous March 7, 1850, speech in the United States Senate, in which Webster addressed the issue of The Union, brought down upon him all the invective of the abolitionists. It also brought Emerson into the political arena.

It is worth mentioning here, at a distance of 150 years, that slavery had never been debated openly in the halls of Congress. As we learn from William Miller's important book, *Arguing About Slavery: The Great Battle in the United States Congress* (Knopf, 1997), the Southern states had forty extra seats in the House because of the three-fifths rule that allowed them to count (but not represent) their slaves, and they had imposed an effective gag rule on any and all mention of slavery on the floors of Congress. In effect, the business of the government was carried on as if slavery did not even exist.

Not only was debate silenced, but Southern representatives and senators spoke away from Washington of the "interest" of slavery as a gift from Providence. It was not until 1836 that John Quincy Adams, having left the Presidency and then been elected to Congress, began using his position and prestige to foment against slavery. His efforts finally ended the gag rule in 1844 and released a torrent of anti-slavery rhetoric into the halls of Congress. When Emerson entered the debate in the furor over the Fugitive Slave Law, many in Congress were grateful for his commitment.

Emerson had always had a clear and straight path to the center of his being. The "Divinity School Address" marks the moment in 1838 when that clarity first appeared in the cause of religious truth and God-knowing. Years later, in the aftermath of Webster's betrayal, the lecture "The Fugitive Slave Law" became a similar clear and direct vision of the same truth.

Emerson's commitment to anti-slavery activism served to punctuate the two essential episodes in his spiritual journey. The "Fugitive Slave Law" is almost as important a spiritual document as the "Divinity School Address." Both were courageous attacks on powerful institutions. The importance of the "Fugitive Slave Law" was not so much its overt attack on Webster himself, as it was the clear characterization of a man without a spiritual center, or, we might say, a moral compass. Its power comes interestingly enough, as did the earlier address, from its confrontation with institutional failure—in both cases represented by Harvard University, the institution which had kept Emerson from its doors for thirty years after the heresies of the Divinity Address.

When Emerson traveled to New York in 1854 to deliver a new version of the "Fugitive Slave Law" address, he changed the concluding portion of the speech to include a reference to the failure of the universities to take a moral stand in time of a national crisis.

> The universities are not, as in Hobbes's time, "the core of rebellion," no but the seat of inertness. They have forgotten their allegiance to the Muse, and have grown worldly and political. I listened, lately, on one of those occasions when the university chooses one of its distinguished sons returning from the political arena, believing that senators and statesmen would be glad to throw off the harness and to dip again in the Castalian pools. But if audiences forget themselves, statesmen do not. The low bow to all the crockery gods of the day were duly made . . .

Emerson's reference to the ancient ritual of making the pilgrimage from the worldly domains of the *agora* to the slopes of godly Delphi, there to purify oneself in the fragrant pools before ascending to the temple of Apollo, stands in sharp contrast to the "seat of inertness" where God no longer dwells. Once within the precincts of the temple, the pilgrim was reminded to "Know Thyself" before he made inquiry of the prophetess to know his fate. Emerson's psychic center was steeped in self-knowing, and even in his vituperation against Webster he maintained a level head and a constant heart.

His final call in "The Fugitive Slave Law" to the people and institutions of America in the crisis of the Union was made not with anger or with even a direct reference to the present circumstances. Rather it came through Romantic imagery meant to evoke a forgotten system of values.

> But I put it to every poetic, every noble, every religious heart, that not so is our learning, our education, our poetry, our worship to be declared. Liberty is aggressive, Liberty is the Crusade of all brave and conscientious men, the Epic Poetry, the new religion, the chivalry of all gentlemen. This is the oppressed Lady whom true knights on their oath and honor must rescue and save.

That day in New York he was addressing the Anti-Slavery Society. At least one purpose of his address, the purpose he could best serve, was to inspire its members for the battle ahead. The invoking of the Crusades and Arthurian legend lends a purity of emotion to the task at hand and anticipates the call to arms to come. In his own prophetic enthusiasm, he knew what was coming and knew that it had to come.

What is also interesting in the passage, however, is the reference to "the new religion." In a speech before the Free Religious Association in 1869, after the blood-letting of the Civil War, Emerson spoke of his hopes for a true spiritual revolution in American worship, one which would evolve and develop without churches.

> We are all very sensible—it is forced on us every day—of the feeling that churches are outgrown; that a technical theology no longer suits us. It is not the ill will of people—no, indeed, but the incapacity for confining themselves there. The church is not large enough for the man; it cannot inspire the enthusiasm which is the parent of everything good in history, which makes the romance of history. For that enthusiasm you must have something greater than yourselves, not less.

To the last, Emerson was primarily interested in expanding the individual's self-knowledge and full potential as a spiritual being. The fame he acquired from his anti-slavery position was unwanted. All his life he had devoted himself to those who were spiritually imprisoned, and yet he had become a name in America on the strength of his moral outrage. He would not have wanted to be confined to the role of America's moral compass. And yet, when he made the incisive comment that as soon as we put a chain around another's neck the other end fastens around our own, he made the crucial connection between the so-called "interest" of slavery and the great law of compensation.

# 12         I AND THE ABYSS

*Stanley Cavell,* in his *In Quest of the Ordinary* (University of Chicago Press, 1988) speaks to the difficulty of belatedly including Emerson in serious philosophical discussion. To his lasting credit, Cavell has gone back from an early interest in Thoreau's *Walden* to examine its roots in Emerson's thinking. As Cavell points out, the bias of American philosophy toward argumentation makes Emerson problematic. Emerson never argued. He observed, reported. Although he refers often enough to his philosophic roots in Coleridge, Kant, and Plato, Emerson seldom quotes them in support of a philosophical position. Instead, he took their "lustres," as he called them, and remained focused on observing his own experience.

If we think for a moment of Porte's image of Emerson as a "tutelary divinity," we begin to see the difficulty of placing him in the philosophic canon. He is regarded as a seer without a pulpit. How do we now place him in the philosophic mainstream to be included in university philosophy courses, or even in the theological debate?

In ten years of teaching Emerson as a philosopher, I always begin by suggesting to students that they take Emerson seriously. In other words, they should read him *as if* he meant what he said: quite literally. I employ the fictive *as if* as a way of sliding into a serious reading. An example of such a slide might be facing the difficulty of the following from "Self-Reliance":

> There is a time in every man's education when he arrives at the conviction that envy is ignorance; that imitation is suicide; that he must take himself for better, for worse, as his portion; that though the wide universe is full of good, no kernel of nourishing corn can

come to him but through his toil bestowed on that plot of ground which is given to him to till. The power which resides in him is new in nature, and none but he knows what that is which he can do, nor does he know until he has tried.

In the context of an academic environment in which students are striving to find a place for themselves in the great western tradition, this passage strongly disturbs the conventional way of thinking—exactly Emerson's pointed intent. What is a student to do with the sentence, "The power which resides in [you] is new in nature . . . ?" Such a truth (as opposed to its reading as a Romantic image of the life-force) shrinks the entire Western canon into a ball or even a black hole and places the student floating in existential space, searching for his or her place to stand. This exact experience for Emerson is recorded in *Nature* and is repeated in a thousand images throughout his work.

Emerson's vision of Being, of human nature, and his fundamental concept of self-reliance constitute a coherent philosophy, even a systematic one if we care to look closely enough. His thought represents an evolution of the mind influenced both by European philosophy and Eastern mysticism and had its birth in the fertile soil of the American experience. His writing emerged from his century and his character, and was honed on the rough wheel of his experience. As such, Emersonian thought was not a minor, Romantic trend in religion or philosophy. Rather, it was an evolutionary mutation of the core of American consciousness, a new thing in nature, and we are who we are as a nation because of it.

Emerson's vision is American in nature because we as Americans have a distinctive sense of Unity within the diversity of our melting-pot culture. European nationalism and class hierarchy are not fertile ground for this kind of thinking. Americans have an instinct for seeing things in wholes despite and because of diversity. We want to arrive in our thinking at some vision of the individual within the Absolute, which is a reason that Indian gurus found such acceptance in America during the Sixties and following decades. The current interest in the Dalai Lama and the struggles of Tibet against Chinese hegemony reflect both our sense of political freedom and our vision of Oneness in seeking religious independence of thought. All of this is Emersonian in character.

If we understand the great chasm or abyss that separates us from the divine ground, our national instinct is to bridge that chasm and not simply to accept it as an inevitable or fundamental separation. We have a national sense of space which understands the abyss and how it may be viewed. The Grand Canyon is our archetypal National Park.

European tradition, on the other hand, accepts otherness and builds religious systems around it. Roman Catholicism, a European export, depends on otherness and builds cathedrals in honor of its permanent character. To enter the unique confines of a cathedral is to meet God as Other because its geometry and monumental size appear as a symbol of Otherness. In America, on the other hand, the great wilderness places the individual alone with God. We understand the abyss and build our bridges accordingly.

More now, needs to be said about the nature of this abyss in Emerson's vision. As Harold Bloom reports in his celebration of Emerson and the American Religion *(Agon,* 1982), Emerson effectively concluded his lifelong journal-keeping in 1866 with a significant comment on his life's work: "There may be two or three or four steps, according to the genius of each, but for every seeing soul there are two absorbing facts,—I and the Abyss." The Abyss for Emerson emerges from a series of sources. One of them is similar to Jacob Boehme's *Urgrund,* the abyss from which God emerges, or the abyss which *is* God. From this Abyss emanates spirit as a force or energy, from which in turn emanates Nature. This conclusion does not necessarily represent a capitulation in Emerson's attempt to achieve a unity of vision. He himself recognized that he existed in a kind of Trinitarian world. First, there was contemplation, then thought, and finally creation—in his case writing. But he was finally more aware of a fundamental duality in his struggle.

The "I" is the Self-reliant mind, the seeker with no past at his back, living in the moment and acting within the stream of power emanating eternally from the Divine Source. It is an aspect of Universal Mind within the human instrument. The other pole, the Abyss, is that chasm of the Infinite and the Unknown, the essential mystery of God-knowing which stimulates our religious longing and philosophical speculations. Its "mind" is the emanated Over-Soul in Emerson's pantheon. To complete the imagery, here is the Abyss in "Compensation":

> Under all this running sea of circumstance, whose waters ebb and flow with perfect balance, lies the aboriginal abyss of real Being. Essence, or God, is not a relation or a part, but the whole.

The equation thus runs Abyss = Being = Essence = God = Whole. It is a circle of aspects. The nature of compensation, or fate, within this whole is that life, or the sea of circumstance, moves in perfect balance *because* the centering Abyss lies silent at the core.

If we were to develop a visionary document with which to study Emerson's relationship to the Abyss more formally, we could assemble a book entitled *I and the Abyss,* which would contain the following published material:

| | |
|---|---|
| The Introduction from *Nature* | Divinity School Address |
| Self-Reliance | Spiritual Laws |
| The Over-Soul | Circles |
| Demonology | Immortality |
| Worship | Natural History of Intellect |

This sequence of essays provides the interested reader with a chronological and systematic vision of Emerson's spiritual thought. It begins with the Introduction from *Nature* because there, in a brief five hundred words, appear the central questions to be answered in the rest of the work. It begins:

> Why should not we also enjoy an original relation to the universe? Why should not we have a poetry and philosophy of insight and not of tradition, and a religion by revelation to us, and not the history of theirs? Embosomed for a season in nature, whose floods of life stream around and through us, and invite us by the powers they supply, to action proportioned to nature, why should we grope among the dry bones of the past, or put the living generation into masquerade out of its faded wardrobe? The sun shines to-day also.

There is more wool and flax in the fields. There are new lands, new men, new thoughts. Let us demand our own works and laws and worship.

The "original relation to the universe" lies in our self-reliant intuition and, if not rejection, at least a careful monitoring of all religious and philosophical formalities. The "philosophy of insight" is the most challenging way to be in the world because we have not been formally taught to rely on our own perceptions. Our education lays stress on accepting the traditions and values of those who have gone before as being more reliable, even if our instinct tells us that what has gone before has not served us well. Educators teach by handing down information, not, alas, by eliciting original thinking from the growing consciousness.

Part of the reason for this imposition of values and standards from which Conservatives think we are fleeing, is the experience of the 1960s. Students then appeared to reject all past values, and the figure of Thoreau came to symbolize the act of intellectual rebellion, of marching to a different drummer. Needless to say, this attraction to Thoreau and his particular Transcendentalism was superficial at best and misunderstood at worst. The dominant theme of the student movement of the Sixties was staying out of the war, not merely rejecting the intellectual standards of the day.

As to Emerson, interest in his thought beginning in the 1970s followed the introduction of Eastern thought into the American culture and prompted an examination of his interest in and devotion to ancient Hindu texts—particularly the Bhagavad-Gita, but also including the ten principal Upanishads and the Laws of Manu. Essays such as *Emerson and Vedanta* by Swami Paramananda are typical of efforts making this connection. The importance of the Eastern influence is to point out Emerson's devotion to Unity as the over-arching principle of his vision.

Our hypothetical text, *I and the Abyss*, illustrates this Eastern connection. It concludes with the late essay "Natural History of Intellect," in which Emerson recapitulates his life's work. His eloquence does not often have the character of summation. Usually it ascends and broadens its circle of influence. Here, however, is summation:

I am of the oldest religion. Leaving aside the question which was prior, egg or bird, I believe the mind is the creator of the world, and is ever creating;—that at last Matter is dead Mind; that mind makes the senses it sees with; that the genius of man is a continuation of the power that made him and has not done making him.

Prior to this conclusion, Emerson warns against the dangers of most metaphysics, particularly of the Eastern variety. He declares that metaphysics has the danger of excessive inward seeking. He warns, "The inward analysis must be connected by rough experience." I wonder, however, if in the light of current experience, in the pervasive infusion of "rough experience" into the very souls of our daily lives, if we might not need to concentrate our attention on pure metaphysics as a balancing exercise. When Emerson warns us that "metaphysics must be perpetually reinforced by life," we are tempted to answer that now life has overwhelmed us with its pervasive intrusions and floods of data. The most disciplined seeker or introspective thinker cannot today find this necessary balance. The need has changed. Indeed the practices of Eastern meditation and detachment have helped millions deal successfully with the ravages of rampant culture. As one contemporary observer has noted, the ordinary mind is like a puppy we are trying to paper-train.[1] As such, it is certainly contemporary culture that elicits such an image.

Perhaps we can call Emerson's vision a Spiritual or Noetic Metaphysics, an anchor or ground to that part of our being which seeks to know the will of God. It is a place to stand. In his youth, in the early journals, Emerson had subtitled his Wide World journals "A Place to Stand," in honor of Archimedes. Emerson found his leverage, in effect, outside the cosmos and simultaneously affirmed that this world is all there is. "Other worlds?" he said, "There are no other worlds." In other words, do not write beyond the limits of rough experience. In that sense, when Harold Bloom claimed that Emerson was always right, he meant that Emerson's texts were always on the subject, always centered. He never tripped on an object and fell on his creative face.

If that is the case, then, how can we talk about Emerson's faith or his trust in the existence and presence of God? The Abyss that marks the polarity with the self-knowing "I" is that Great Unknown into which we cast our longing and our faith. Emerson lived in the abysmal in-between, that space where human mind meets Eternal Mind. He took dictation from that space and reported what he heard there. Although he claimed never to have heard or read or spoken the truth, because such purity could never be perceived directly, he did know that some semblance of the truth breached the space from the Abyss to his mind. That in-between, also known by Plato as the *Metaxy,* is the place where the devout linger in moments of peace and bliss.

The *metaxy* may be described as the middle ground in the relation of I and the Abyss. It is the root of human transformation, and its borders are breached by the power of *eros.* Support for this view comes from the philosopher of history Eric Voegelin. The following comes from his book *Anamnesis,* which takes its title from Plato's examination of remembrance or recollection. Voegelin refers to the *metaxy* as the source of noetic exegesis, which in turn is the only proper ground for the philosopher to explore.

Voegelin's analysis of the *metaxy* begins with Plato and the references to it in the *Symposium* and the *Philebus.* In *Anamnesis,* using a compact language designed to instigate as well as explicate, Voegelin describes the new order as follows:

> Man experiences himself as tending beyond his human imperfection toward the perfection of the divine ground that moves him. The spiritual man . . . as he is moved in his quest of the ground, moves somewhere between knowledge and ignorance. "The whole realm of the spiritual . . . is halfway indeed between (*metaxy*) god and man" (*Symp.* 202a). Thus, the in-between—the *metaxy*—is not an empty space between the poles of the tension but the "realm of the spiritual"; it is the reality of "man's converse with the gods" (202–203), the mutual participation . . . of human in divine, and divine in human, reality. The *metaxy* symbolizes the experience of the noetic quest as a transition of the psyche from mortality to immortality.[2]

The first essential point of this description is that human nature is moved, by the imperfection in which it finds itself, toward the perfection of the divine ground. Our sense of imperfection comes not only from our own internal imperfections (seen as sin or disobedience in religious terms) but also from the imperfections (the dead matter to which Emerson refers above) of the world in which we must live. A fundamental rebellion from this imperfect world serves as an instigator to the seeking spirit and also manifests itself in the artistic impulse as well as in social and political action, such as Emerson's slavery activism.

The other essential point of Voegelin's description of the *metaxy* is that it is indeed "the realm of the spiritual." This distinction between the spiritual realm and the divine ground provides a substantial realm within which the human being may approach and discover a field of participation—in other words, a place to stand. Emerson's discovery of that place is what gave direction and focus for his life and work.

Speaking about those who live and work in the *metaxy* or realm of the spiritual, Voegelin makes the following observation:

> Men do not all have the same spiritual rank. There are the select ones . . . to whom revelations occur, and there is the great mass of mortals who would grope in eternal darkness if God did not from time to time stir up the "highest virtues" in some particular persons so that they can point out the right road to their fellow beings. . . . They [the select] are slandered, exiled, killed, and punished as subverters. Even when their message becomes socially effective, it soon is distorted by superstition, when the historical-human form of revelation is taken for its essence, and fanatical literalists obscure its function, i.e., the purification of the spirit and the turning of the soul to God.[3]

Emerson may be included among the select, or at the very least is an adept observer of the select, seen in his Representative Men. Certainly he suffered the rejection Voegelin describes, and we may easily claim that Emerson suffered a form of martyrdom for his vision. After 1838, he lived outside the pale of New England society as represented by the cultural institutions of Boston and Cambridge.

Was Emerson a "select one?" Certainly he made no claim to such. In fact, his vision always had its foundation in denying to any one person a special relationship to the divine ground. In "Demonology," one of the essays I would include in a Spiritual Emerson text, he establishes a firm principle of judgment in these matters.

> The lovers of marvels, of what we call the occult and unproved sciences, of mesmerism, of astrology, of coincidences, of intercourse, by writing or rapping or by painting, with departed spirits, need not reproach us with incredulity because we are slow to accept their statement. It is not the incredibility of the fact, but a certain want of harmony between the action and the agents.

The "want of harmony" reaches out to all such low miracles that bend the laws of nature and distort our experience. In our efforts to seek evidence of "other worlds," we find instead a severe betrayal of cosmic law. What is harmonic is what is lawful and contained in the light, and it is accessible to all. The demonic, on the other hand, "chooses favorites and works in the dark . . . as if the laws of the Father of the universe were sometimes balked and eluded by a meddlesome Aunt of the universe . . . " Finally, he makes an observation that places the issue firmly at our feet: "The history of man is a series of conspiracies to win from Nature some advantage without paying for it." In spiritual matters, too, there is no free lunch. The godly Emerson asks us, "What do you want? Pay for it and take it!"

What we begin to understand from Emerson's careful reading of occult influences and spiritual desires is that we find true Spirit in our sanity and health. Sanity and health together equal bliss, that state in which clarity of mind reaches across the chasm to truth. Another quality of that state of bliss is immediacy. We are in the moment. For Emerson, being in the moment while at the same time keeping his proverbial wits about him—that is, in a state of reflective self-awareness—meant that the act of thinking and the act of writing took place in the same moment.

This observation comes from Stanley Cavell in a recent book by Giovanna Borradori, entitled *The American Philosopher* (University of Chicago Press, 1994). In answer to a question about Thoreau's *Walden,*

Cavell credits Thoreau with collapsing the entire edifice of Cavell's own early thought. This collapse came when Cavell realized the intent in *Walden*, which is to prove that great writing and thinking happen simultaneously.[4] What does such a statement imply about Emerson and the abyss of gnostic discovery?

If we take a relevant passage from Emerson's most important and influential essay, "Self-Reliance," we may find a clue to this critical philosophical simultaneity. Here is the passage, with italics mine:

> The *other terror* that scares us from self-trust is our consistency; a reverence for our past act or word, because the eyes of others have no other data for *computing our orbit* than our past acts, and we are loath to disappoint them.
>
> But why should you keep your head over your shoulder? Why drag about this *corpse of your memory*, lest you contradict somewhat you have stated in this or that public place? Suppose you should contradict yourself; what then? It seems to be a rule of wisdom never to rely on your memory alone, scarcely even in acts of pure memory, but to bring the past for judgment into *the thousand-eyed present*, and live ever in a new day. In your metaphysics you have denied personality to the Deity: yet when the *devout motions of the soul* come, yield to them *heart and life*, though they should *clothe God* with shape and color. *Leave your theory, as Joseph his coat in the hand of the harlot, and flee.*

The constant surprise of startling images in these sentences, in spite of the coherence of the overall argument, pulls us away from our foolish consistency, the hobgoblin of our chattering little minds, and instigates in us a more conscious reading. We are stimulated to give quality attention. The eye is constantly shocked with the appearance of orbits, corpses, and thousand-eyed presents. These images come, as Emerson himself described, from pictures that leapt to his mind in the moments of transmission. There was the world in orbit, there the corpse of memory, there the ferocious multi-eyed moment in which the ego might be devoured, never to return. And despite our metaphysics, our analysis of the abstract God, the Great Universal Force, we find in our hearts a God in our own image, the grandfather of our dreams who comforts us or saves us from the deceit of Potiphar's wife.

The mixing of metaphors, breaking the rules of writing at every turn, also keeps us vitally engaged. From looking over our shoulders as we run in terror, dragging our corpses, to images of Yahweh in the desert, our senses are shaken. Life is presented to us as a violent crisis where our very lives are at stake, and yet, all we are ostensibly talking about is foolish consistency. Emerson is telling us that the act of transformation to the upright position of self-trust is freedom from the nightmares of a life lived in the memory. Such a freedom lies in the Infinite.

As most of the biographers have told us, Emerson knew well about the corpses of memory. When his young wife Ellen died on February 8, 1831, she was buried in the family tomb in Roxbury, Massachusetts. Emerson visited as often as he could over the course of a year. Thirteen months after her death, on March 29, 1832, Emerson made this note in his journal: "I visited Ellen's tomb & opened the coffin."[5] Those who feel that this note is metaphoric or came to him in a dream have to contend with the fact of the same action in 1857 when the coffin of little Waldo Emerson was being moved, fifteen years after the boy's death, to the new Sleepy Hollow Cemetery. Before the coffin was lowered to its new resting place, Emerson asked the caretaker to open the coffin.

These may be morbid, forbidding facts, but Emerson treated himself severely in all matters of memory and sentimental clinging to the past. To see the waste of dead matter in this world helped to wrench him free of the domination of memory and to affirm the principles by which he wished to live his life. His fading memories of loved ones, long gone from the vitality of the living, was for him "the other terror that scares us from self-trust." In a similar, perhaps less gruesome way, I have felt the soft, gritty ash of a loved one soon after holding the flesh in life. It was a healing.

Finally, Emerson makes note in this passage of the demands of the heart in matters of faith and belief. He urges us to flee our metaphysics when "the devout motions of the soul" demand an image for our comfort, or when a crisis makes it necessary to flee from our theories in the face of rude experience. Our refusal to do so marks a foolish consistency and a failure to understand the dual nature of our existence.

In the introduction of this study, I called upon William James to characterize the impact of Emerson's thought on a new century. What he said, in summation, was this:

> For Emerson, the individual fact and moment were indeed suffused with absolute radiance, but it was upon a condition that saved the situation—they must be worthy specimens,—sincere, authentic, archetypal;

These three qualities—sincere, authentic, archetypal—triangulate the body of Emerson's work and give it stability.

For the sake of this new yet unapproachable America of the new millennium, the presence of a sincere, authentic, and archetypal God in Concord is more crucial for our health and survival than is a God in Jerusalem, Rome, Dallas, or Salt Lake City. I do not mean, of course, that we should worship Emerson—a man who spent his life telling us not to follow much less worship him. I mean we should emulate his high degree of self-trust. As Bloom has said, we are thankful there is no Emersonian Church. I do not mean either that we should found some kind of Unchurch of the Cosmic Mind and worship there, because—if history is accurate—we shall soon have the Church of the Cosmic Mind in actual locations, with rituals of worship. It was Kafka who noted in one of his paradoxes that at night leopards enter the temple to drink from the sacrificial waters. Soon, their entry can be predicted in advance and becomes part of the ceremony. Properly, then, the idea of a God in Concord places us in that in-between space, the *metaxy* or realm of the spiritual where the self-examined life is led and known in solitary advances toward the infinite.

If it is true, as some predict, that professional philosophy is finally being returned to the public arena after nearly a century of closet debating; and if theological and biblical studies are seeing more of the light of day, released to the public from their confinement in elite scholarly darkness; if all this is true, we may soon see a true ecumenical movement among worshippers away from narrow sectarianism and toward a genuine community of self-recovery.

It is doubtful, however, that such recovery can happen within institutions. The tendency of churchmen is still to hold stubbornly to doctrinal differences. After all, if the Mormons (whom Bloom feels will soon inherit the earth) are succeeding in their recruitment efforts, why should they change their formula? And what is formula except doctrine? This stubbornness plagues Jews as well, despite the fact that their doctrinal differences, especially among the branches of the Orthodox, have spilled out of the synagogues into the streets, with the effect that more and more people are seeing these doctrinal disputes, among Jews and Christians alike, as alienating and pointless. As Emerson said, questions concerning the anatomy of angels never presented a practical problem for anyone. Some, of course, find solace in a narrow truth, convinced that their religion is authentic and all others are clever counterfeits. It seems to make the simple-minded content to feel they have a small piece of the truth that billions of others do not share at their eternal peril.

Statistics, for what they are worth, tell a different story. People seem not to join churches because they are attracted to doctrine. They join to be with people like themselves. They are searching for comfort and security. As soon as they feel uncomfortable or insecure, they leave and search for another place to feel comfortable. This is Church as Repose. What these people actually believe in their heart of hearts is another matter.

What Emerson constantly urges is the search for the peace that can come only from self-realized observation and knowledge. He even pictured himself going from door to door describing, to anyone who would listen, the bliss he enjoyed as a solitary believer. But to do so, of course, would be to deny the very process that gave birth to the bliss in the first place.

In her conversation with Stanley Cavell in *The American Philosopher*, Borradori arrives, as we arrive, at the same place:

BORRADORI: From Christ, once again to Emerson.

CAVELL: Yes, because he is the philosopher who contradicts Heidegger's effort to dwell by saying that you have to leave. Abandonment is for me the first door. You abandon the word you write, the house you live in, your father and mother, your sister and brother. You have to leave when the kingdom of heaven calls you. But what's the kingdom of heaven? Emerson pictures it as writing, which in turn he will abandon only for thinking. So, in this sense of abandoning things and moving on, Emerson is a Jew, Thoreau is a Jew, and I'm a Jew. Or at least I would like to become one.

Another way of putting this is that we are all part of the Great Diaspora, set free from deadly tradition and the boundaries of race, religion, and even culture to become children of the planet . . . or the universe. Witness how the Jewish religion became more subtle and mature as a result of the enslavement in Babylon. If a myth or a tradition is able to expand to these dimensions, then it may have a place in our journey. If not, it must be abandoned. Whatever has in it an archetypal power may still serve our journey. What has none will not.

Emerson's abandonment was the escape from false ties and the courage to be what he was and might become. Writing was the proper expression of his genius. In it, he continued his abandonment by insisting on being true to his moments of inspiration, wherever they led. His refusal to debate the issues that emerged from his writing was his affirmation of their authenticity. When approached after a lecture by those who wished to take issue with a point, he would say that if anything in the talk met a need or spoke to the heart of a listener, that was all he could hope for, but he would not speak to particulars. This loyalty to the intuitive process meant that if someone did wish to question a particular, it was obvious that they were not listening in the same spirit.

Nothing is more difficult than abandonment in this sense. The key passage in "Self-Reliance" (already quoted in chapter 10) is a necessary severity:

Your goodness must have some edge to it, else it is none. The doctrine of hatred must be preached as the counteraction of the doctrine of love when that pules and whines. I shun father and mother and wife and brother, when my genius calls me. I would write on the lintels of the door-post, "Whim." I hope it is somewhat better than whim at last, but we cannot spend the day in explanation.

Here is Emerson at his very best: unsentimental, even shocking, but always right. Others have pointed out the reference to the Passover theme in the "lintels of the door-post." If there is validity to the myth, then it must pass the test of authenticity. Emerson's use here of biblical allusion illustrates the proper role of myth. Here we are told that protection from the powers of darkness, from death itself, is found only in obedience to the genius which calls. To do anything else—to explain, to justify, even to love when it "pules and whines"—is deadly.

We all hope, of course, that our abandonment is better than Whim at last, but we can never be sure. The abyss is there, always, and no materialistic reductionism will ever explain it away. The universe is wide and deep. Emerson tells us that when we abandon our false props (or propositions) our minds are just as wide and just as deep. And identity is the vanishing point of resemblance.

# EMERSON'S LEGACY

*At the Bicentennial* Celebration of Emerson's birth, which as noted earlier will take place in May, 2003, the question will no doubt arise: "What is the strength and importance of Emerson's legacy for the new millennium?" The thrust of this book has been to provide an impulse in the direction of answering that question.

Some contemporary thinkers—those in philosophy, science, and theology, for example—tend to consign Transcendental Idealism to the storage cabinet as an extinct historical curiosity. As it existed as an "ism," I tend to agree. It may well belong with Communism and existentialism as an intellectual and social movement that no longer has a role on the contemporary stage. On the other hand, Emerson's vision as encapsulated in his work is another matter entirely. What he had to say—specifically about the effort of human beings to recover their humanity from the effects of materialism's rampage across the American nineteenth-century landscape—has abundant vitality for our own reductive postmodernist age.

As thinking, feeling human beings, we have intimations of the accuracy of Emerson's observations. If we are fortunate, we also have personal experiences of our own which tend to verify them. These intimations fly in the face of what we call "rational" thought and the thrust of twentieth-century philosophy which in its concern with language, focused its substantial resources on epistemology. The victories of the Vienna Circle in the 1920s effectively dismissed ontology from our concerns as philosophers, with Wittgenstein completing that cycle by declaring in the *Tracticus* that what couldn't be discussed shouldn't be discussed. It was an endgame.

*Emerson in 1874*

By the close of this century, however, a new impulse has entered the arena in the form of the mind/brain problem. Efforts to explain the intricate, complex, and contradictory activities of human thought have opened the door to a new depth of inquiry. Epistemology by itself is inadequate to the task. Philosophy has properly joined the discussion, and the new depth of thought lends fresh credibility to those thinkers, led by Emerson, whose work overtly examined an unbounded potential of human imagination and insight.

For modern philosophy to fully enter this arena once again, however, it must find fresh ways to investigate the metaphysical landscape it abandoned a hundred years ago. Surely, there exists a formulation for making ontological statements that reveal and explore heretofore unknown realms of reality in which consciousness is found to exist outside of the strict confines of human biology. That, after all, was Emerson's essential claim.

It was never Emerson's intent to project into Nature a new God-like human entity that would be the measure of all things. Messiah hunters beware. He was interested in human self-recovery, in restoring to *every* human being a measure of the strength and insight to which our natural evolution entitles us. In his vision human beings are not *essentially* flawed, but he saw clearly that in the mythus of Christianity, indeed in all religions, imposing a hierarchal order stifles our natural powers. While still supporting the efforts of religion to prevent the terrors of oppression and the horrors of genocide (as opposed to fostering them), Emerson nonetheless demanded that religion also work to free the human mind and heart from authoritarian controls.

Emerson spoke to release individuals from spiritual prisons of all kinds. His vision celebrates the ability and right of each individual human being to reach freely into the infinite resources of nature for life-enhancing knowledge and power. His vision does not tend toward the withering away of established religion or propose some Ayn Randian exaltation of the personal ego. Emerson always affirmed that Self-Reliance is God-Reliance, as Harold Bloom has reminded us. Religion as an institution, like government, still has efficacy as a part of civilization. That it needs constant renewal and leadership from enlightened human minds is just as clear.

The knowledge and power we are free to discover in the core of nature is universal, not personal. At the core exists a matrix of causal reality, a logos of triune forces lawfully holding the universe together, emanating immense energy which is available for our use. This matrix contains the substance of consciousness, the stuff of stars, and the essence of the biological existence we call life. Seers like Emerson have tapped into that matrix for our benefit. In Emerson's individual, historical case an intuitive idealism and an exhilarating eloquence surged forth which, with some help, will survive as long as it continues to nurture the human condition.

# EPILOGUE

*In the early 1860s,* at a point in his life when he had seen himself waning in strength—indeed even dreamed once that he had fallen asleep while lecturing—Emerson took the time to jot down in his notebooks the essentials of his journey as a seeker. It was an exercise in review and recollection. In notebook DL, in use from 1860 through 1866, he noted what he called "The Memorabilia of philosophy," those ideas and statements which were for him most worthy of recollection. These were:

Plato's doctrine of Reminiscence

Berkeley's Ideal World

Socrates' interpretation of the Delphian oracle[1]

The Dance of Plotinus

Doctrine of Absorption [*Nirvana*]

Greek saying, that the soul is absorbed into God as a phial of water broken in the sea

Plotinus's saying: "There however every body is pure, (transparent), and each inhabitant is as it were an eye."

Heraclitus said: "War is the father of all things."

"A dry light makes the best soul."

"Like can only be known by like."

"*Nec sentire deum nisi qui pars ipse deorum est.*" ["Only if a man be himself the infinite, can the infinite be known by him."]

"*Ne te quaesiveris extra.*" (Persius, *Satires,* I,7) ["Look to no one outside yourself."]

"*Natura in minimus existit.*" (Aristotle) ["... the nature of everything
is best seen in its smallest proportions."] trans. Francis Bacon

Hunger & thirst after righteousness. (Matt. 5:6)

Kingdom of God cometh not by observation. (Luke 17:20)

... is received as a little child (Luke 18:17)

Christianity, pure deism

God considers integrity not munificence. (Socrates)

These references appear elsewhere in the journals and notebooks on
multiple occasions and were no doubt culled as an exercise in essentials. For us, the value is in seeing both the sequence and the significance
as a kind of talisman of the journey. These are the major "lustres" of a
lifetime of reading and contemplation.

PLATO'S DOCTRINE OF REMINISCENCE. The essential metaphysical fact
for Emerson is the presence within each human being of primary spiritual knowledge, Plato's *anamnesis,* or reminiscence. As the Hindu texts
of Vedanta tell us, we promise at birth to remember who we are and
to return to our Creator. The primary truth, *tat twam asi,* or "That
Thou Art," marks the identification of the small, personal self with the
larger, infinite Self. We know we are the Self and we see that same Self
in everything. Emerson's Self-reliance always refers to this greater Self
to make that affirmation clear. Life is a journey of returning, through
reminiscence, to the source. We are to remember ourselves.

BERKELEY'S IDEAL WORLD. The journey is made possible by the knowledge argued by George Berkeley in *A Treatise Concerning the Principles
of Human Knowledge:* Matter is illusory and the perceiving mind is
capable, therefore, of acquiring knowledge of the transparent reality
which includes the Infinite. In daily life, while we are at play with the
sense objects of existence, it is easy to forget ourselves, to become lost
in the habitual round of events and sensations. The implications for
Emerson were, therefore, that consciousness, which is pivotal to human
existence, is indeed the only reality, since the perceived world, or mat-

ter, is a function of consciousness and not separate from perception. This is "Ideal" because we are not, therefore, presented with "the way things are" as Hume would have it, but rather we may, through conscious effort, come to know Universal Mind, which stands behind the sense objects and is their source. Berkeley's idealism is really immaterialism and coincides with the Indian Sanskrit idea of Maya as envisioned by Shankara in Advaita Vedanta.

THE DANCE OF PLOTINUS. There are several possibilities for the "Dance" of Plotinus. The first may be a reference to what Plotinus called the Cosmic Circuit: the constant circular motion of matter in harmony, with the silent, unmoving Soul at the center. This image maintains the independence of the Great Soul from mixture with the matter of the universe. Also, and more interesting in terms of Emerson's personal vision of correspondences within nature of the universal principles within human nature, is a reference from a commentary by Marcilio Ficino, the famous Italian Renaissance classical scholar and gnostic seer. Ficino was himself commenting on a commentary by Proclus. In fact, there are so many levels here that we have to go back to regroup for a moment.

First, as noted in Chapter Nine, Emerson knew Plato and the Neoplatonists through Thomas Taylor. The primary text Emerson knew was Taylor's five-volume translation of Plato, published in 1804. The first dialogue in Volume One is *The First Alcibiades*. There Taylor says Proclus called this dialogue "the most peculiar and firm principle of all the dialogues of Plato." Its primary subject is a description of the attributes of human nature; central to that nature is the existence of the *daemon* as the divine essence of our existence.

In Emerson's personal copy of Taylor's *Plotinus,* Emerson marked several passages of Ficino's commentary, including this one pertaining to the hierarchy of motions in nature and their relationship to the divine source.

> For how shall we account for those plants called heliotropes, that is, attendants on the sun, moving in correspondence with the revolution of its orb . . . ? It is because all things pray, and hymn the leaders of their respective orders; but some intellectually, and

others rationally; some in a natural and others after a sensible, manner. Hence the sunflower, as far as it is able, moves in a circular dance toward the sun; so that if any one could hear the pulsation made by its circuit in the air, he would perceive something composed by a sound of this kind, in honor of its king, such as a plant is capable of framing.[2]

Finding this correspondence with the great Cosmic dance in the subtle motions of plants, (*Natura in minimus existit*), combined with the image of prayer and the intellectual action of language as a theotropic movement, was for Emerson the kind of connective and unifying symbolism central to his own temperament and imagination. His admiration of both Goethe and Swedenborg was founded on their systems of correspondence, which Emerson extended to language itself in the tropes formed between his mental imagery and his grammar. In the same journal entry devoted to the memorabilia of philosophy, he made a reference to the word "like" in consideration of the functions of Imagination:

> Note our incessant use of the word: *like* a pelican pecking her breast to feed her young, *like* a horse always at the end of his tether, Athens which has lost her young men is *like* a year without a spring.[3]

**DOCTRINE OF ABSORPTION (*NIRVANA*).** This doctrine speaks to Emerson's ideas about immortality. The image of the soul being absorbed into God as a phial of water broken in the sea, is the Nirvana of the Eastern traditions. That the personality does not survive in absorption was not a concern for Emerson. He could not imagine how the collection of memories, thoughts, and peculiarities could survive the death of the body. In "Immortality" he suggested simply that if it were best that the personality survive, then it would. Certainly, he parted company with aspects of Christian belief in this matter, although he made the observation that nowhere does Jesus make any reference to personal immortality.

**PLOTINUS' SAYING.** The reference to *Plotinus' saying* "There however every body is pure, (transparent), and each inhabitant is as it were an eye" is strongly suggestive of the famous Transparent Eyeball image from *Nature*. The first reference to that image appears in Emerson's journal for March, 1835, and we know that he had been reading Taylor's works, including the *Plotinus,* since 1831.[4] It is highly likely that this image, remembered in the 1860s, served to frame the experience of transparency from *Nature*. The intent had been to describe a transcendent experience on a bare common in twilight as an intuitive source of knowing. In order for the ego to recede and for the mind to perceive purely in that rare moment of understanding, the image of the transparent eye renders the idea accurately.

HERACLITUS. Emerson's admiration for Heraclitus was of long standing. The three references from the fragments reflect three distinct interests: the theory of compensation (the image of war), the purity of one's life being necessary to know God (the dry soul), and the state of one's soul being the determining factor in its fate (like to like). Two of the fragments relate to the role of strife or war in creation and sustaining life. These are:

> It is necessary to know that warfare is universal and that strife is right, and that all things happen through strife and necessity.

> War is the father of All That Is and king of All That Is, and some participants he shows as immortal, others as mortal; some he makes slaves, others free.

Emerson's vision of compensation, fate, necessity, and destiny all coincide with these assertions. "Strife is right" extends to both natural and human conflict. Abrasion makes fire, which brings light into the darkness. So too with philosophical issues. As Jesus brought fire and sword, so too Emerson saw himself as of the party of reform opposing the establishment. That he chose always to avoid argument marks his distinction between personal and cosmic strife. He always believed that there is nothing we can do to solve the times. Only on the issue of slavery did he enter the fray out of conscience.

The image of the dry soul in Heraclitus is more complex. Readers familiar with the humours of Hippocrates may have some familiarity with the ancient study of dry and moist souls. The fragments relating to these factors are three:

> It is death for souls to become water, as it is death for water to become earth; water comes to be from earth, as soul comes from water.

> A dry soul is wisest and best.

> When he is drunk, thus having his soul moist, a man is led about by an immature boy, stumbling and not knowing where he is going.

We can glean from these images some sense in which the idea of a dry soul is desirable. Heraclitus used fire as his image of consciousness and as the foundational element of the cosmos. The Logos, so central to Heraclitus, could only be known through the fire of waking consciousness. Finally, the idea of "like can only be known by like," comes less from Heraclitus and more from Marie Gerando and from Coleridge. The Gerando reads, "Le même ne peut être conçu que par le même"[5] and is derived from Aristotle. The statement from Coleridge appears in his *The Statesman's Manual*.[6]

The fire that is Emerson's passion for the truth, the like to be known by like, finds its perfect expression in "Immortality": "Only if a man be himself the infinite, can the infinite by known by him." The approach to godliness in humility, terror, courage, and daring filled Emerson with the power of eloquence, despite what he saw as physical weakness and a lack of personal warmth. In the "Address" he said, "If a man is at heart just, then in so far is he God." His "in so far" takes the human condition to the edge of the abyss, but no further. Later in the same essay he said, speaking for Jesus, "Would you see God, see me; or, see thee, when thou also thinkest as I now think."

We come close to God when we speak for God. If "Man is a god in ruins," what is the course of our self-recovery if not approach to self-recovery in words and actions? It is this meaning in which Emerson includes the traditional admonition to "hunger and thirst after righteousness." Elsewhere he noted that a whole new era began in human history in the light of this clarion call.

CHRISTIANITY, PURE DEISM. By way of summarizing this study, we can make an observation or two about "Christianity pure deism." Emerson's deism parallels the beliefs of the English Deists of the eighteenth century (and to some extent Voltaire in France) in rejecting superstition, super-naturalism, and external revelation. He had read Voltaire on and off since 1825, and among the English Deists he knew of Herbert of Cherbury (1583–1648), usually thought of as the founder of Deism. The Deists rejected Christianity's claim to be the only source of salvation and compiled articles common to all world religions. This assertion that Jesus Christ is the (only) Way, the Truth and the Life, is seen by Christians as the proof of its unique (and thus superior) status, requiring therefore the spread of its influence to all nations. Emerson's rejection of this exclusivity makes him, in some minds, a non-Christian.

It is difficult to imagine as we enter the twenty-first century and survive the millennial madness, that mainstream Christianity will continue its claims for exclusivity in matters of salvation, thus maintaining its superstitions. As a religion, Christianity can take its place among the religions of the world as an advocate for the existence of God, for human dignity and economic justice, and be a force to counteract the excesses of exploitive economics and the spread of rampant materialism. It can also, and in some enlightened ways already has, become a spiritual setting in which individuals come into a unity of community in order to experience God. This more esoteric purpose has long held a small but vibrant place in its ethos.

Emerson's place in the history of Christianity should no longer be seen as an heretical interlude but rather as a movement toward a New Deism. The new articles of such a deism, partly derived from Herbert's original articles, might be: a) God exists; b) it is our nature to seek God and what God is; c) the extent to which we approach God's attributes, we approach God; d) we are forever responsible for our actions; and by implication, e) our ultimate destiny, whatever that might be, is dependent upon our actions in this life. To the extent that these articles are subversive are they also true.

It is certainly true that the voice of Emerson, our God in Concord, seems a mere murmur in the cacophony of contemporary experience. But his original pleas in "The Address" still echo through the empty canyons of our present abyss. Emerson must have felt about his talk that July day in 1838 what Lincoln felt at Gettysburg, that few would note or long remember his remarks. Rather than spoken just to a half dozen members of the class, their guests and faculty, "The Address" marked the beginning of a new era in the progress of the soul in the "matter" we call America. As Emerson said, it is spiritual food for those who are starving in the midst of plenty.

It is time that this ill-suppressed murmur of all thoughtful men against the famine of our churches; this moaning of the heart because it is bereaved of the consolation, the hope, the grandeur, that come alone out of the culture of the moral nature; should be heard through the sleep of indolence, and over the din of routine.

# NOTES

## INTRODUCTION

1. James, William, *Essays in Religion and Morality*. Harvard University Press, Cambridge, 1982, p. 114.

## CHAPTER 1

1. Usually thought of as the doctrine of the personal God in opposition to pantheism, the doctrine of the impersonal God identified with the universe.
2. JMN, V, 471
3. JMN V, 475
4. JMN V, 477
5. JMN V, 506
6. JMN V, 506
7. JMN V, 507
8. The second floor chapel seats barely one hundred persons. the front pews were occupied by the faculty of the Divinity School, including the retired Andrews Norton, author of *The Evidences of the Genuineness of the Gospels*.
9. JMN V, 463
10. Bloom, p. 24
11. The "fruits of the spirit" characteristic of charismatic congregations take their biblical authority from Acts, Chapter 2, known as the Pentecost. The Holy Spirit descended upon the members of the early Jerusalem Church and they "began to speak with other tongues," and as Peter then testified, "your sons and daughters shall prophesy." (Acts 2, verses 4 and 17, King James version)
12. JMN V, 235
13. Even Emerson's Aunt Mary said that the address had been conceived "under the influence of a malign demon." (Rusk, p. 270)
14. When Emerson resigned from his post at the Second Church six years earlier, his friend and supporter Frederick Hedge had reported to Emerson rumors that society in Boston questioned Emerson's sanity (Rusk, p. 167).
15. JMN VII, 43
16. JMN VII, 39
17. Milton R. Konvitz, *The Recognition of Ralph Waldo Emerson*, University of Michigan Press, 1972, pp. 14–15

## CHAPTER 2

1. Konvitz, p. 15

2. *The American Newness,* Harvard University Press, Cambridge, 1986
3. Shattuck, Roger, *Forbidden Knowledge,* Harcourt Brace, New York, 1997
4. Cavell, Stanley, Cambridge University Press, Cambridge, 1976
5. Cavell, p. xix
6. Cavell, p. 64
7. *Critique of Pure Reason,* trans., N.K. Smith, p. 96
8. Cavell, p. 168
9. An examination of these movements swirling around Emerson can be found in Joscelyn Godwin's lively and thorough *The Theosophical Enlightenment* (SUNY Press, 1994).
10. JMN XIV, 109
11. *The American Religion,* 41

## CHAPTER 3

1. JMN I, 51
2. Below this passage is the phrase "Vide Price on Morals," no doubt referring to "decisions of the understanding."
3. JMN I, 261–262
4. JMN II, 87
5. JMN III, 308
6. JMN II, 100
7. Works, v. III, 130 . James Munroe and Company, Boston, 1841
8. JMN II, 136–137
9. JMN II, 140
10. JMN II, 224–225
11. JMN I, 293–294
12. Richardson, 382
13. Carlyle-Emerson Letters, I, 32–33
14. Reed, 9–10.
15. *Agon,* 148
16. JMN III, 60

## CHAPTER 4

1. Geldard, *The Esoteric Emerson,* Lindisfarne Press, 1993
2. JMN III, 117
3. JMN III, 76
4. JMN III, 77
5. JMN III, 77
6. JMN III, 78
7. JMN III, 111–112
8. JMN III, 263, n.
9. JMN III, 192
10. JMN III, 179
11. JMN III, 178
12. JMN III, 182

13. JMN III, 226
14. JMN III, 226
15. JMN III, 235–236
16. JMN III, 236
17. JMN III, 236
18. JMN III, 263, n. 109
19. JMN III, 304
20. JMN IV, 27
21. JMN IV, 28

## CHAPTER 5

1. JMN IV, 126
2. JMN IV, 242
3. JMN IV, 83
4. JMN IV, 84
5. JMN IV, 309
6. JMN IV, 309
7. JMN IV, 313
8. Oliver Wendell Holmes, *Emerson.* Chelsea House, New York, 1980, xvii. (Joel Porte, introduction)
9. JMN IV, 313
10. JMN IV, 313–314
11. JMN IV, 357
12. JMN IV, 372
13. JMN IV, 372
14. JMN IV, 373

## CHAPTER 6

1. JMN IV, 138
2. JMN V, 38
3. JMN V, 38
4. JMN V, 49
5. JMN V, 52
6. JMN V, 77–78. The image of the phial breaking into the sea also appears later among Emerson's "Memorabilia of philosophy" (JMN XV, 6) and is a seminal image in his metaphysics.
7. JMN V, 79
8. JMN V, 84
9. JMN V, 112
10. JMN V, 162–163
11. JMN V, 163
12. JMN V, 169
13. JMN V, 170
14. *Nature,* W I

15. JMN V, 179
16. JMN V, 186
17. JMN V, 187, see Luke 17:21
18. JMN V, 219–220
19. JMN V, 220
20. JMN V, 223
21. JMN V, 223
22. *The Gospel According to Thomas,* Harper and Row, 1959, p. 3
23. JMN IV, 16
24. JMN V, 230

## CHAPTER 7

1. JMN VII, 167–168
2. "Literary Ethics" and also JMN V, 458
3. JMN V, 307
4. JMN V, 307
5. JMN V, 391
6. JMN V, 445–446
7. Jerusalem Bible, Job, 40:6–10
8. "Plato," Emerson's essay
9. JMN V, 305
10. JMN V, 302–303
11. JMN V, 445
12. TN, I, 154 (Also TN II, 186, 233)
13. JMN II, 189–190. Note: the image of mother in this passage parallels a passage from Plotinus in the Fourth Ennead, Third Tractate, paragraph 7, as follows: "As for the fact that we are begotten inside the universe, in the womb too we say that the soul which comes into the child is another one, not that of the mother." (*Plotinus*, Harvard University Press, Loeb Classical Library, volume IV, 55). It is unclear from the record that Emerson had read Plotinus this early in his education, but the similarity is impressive.
14. EL III, 285
15. EL III, 285

## CHAPTER 8

1. JMN IV, 324
2. JMN VII, 342
3. Karl Marx, *The German Ideology,* trans. Tucker, p. 154–55.
4. JMN VII, 450
5. JMN IX, 139
6. JMN VII, 253–254
7. JMN VII, 254
8. JMN VII, 255
9. JMN VII, 255

10. The Jesus Seminar has its base in Santa Rosa, California, at the Westar Institute led by Robert Funk and John Crossan. It has as its stated purpose the continuing research into the life and words of Jesus.

11. The work of the Mother as found in the writings of Sri Aurobindo is a vivid example of this level of transformation.

## CHAPTER 9

1. Uncollected Writings, "The Editors to the Reader," *The Dial*
2. JMN VII, 243
3. JMN VII, 489–490
4. L. II, 399–400
5. The entry for Taylor in the *Dictionary of National Biography* is essentially dismissive. Current scholarship owes much to the renovating work on Taylor by the poet Kathleen Raine.
6. *Select Works of Plotinus,* Thomas Taylor, trans., London, 1817, lxxi. (This edition, from the personal library of Emerson, is now at the Houghton Library of Harvard University.)
7. It is instructive that Orientalists who write about Emerson—such as Swami Paramananda in his *Emerson and Vedanta* (Vedanta Center Publishers, 1918) tend to think of Emerson as a *Bodhisattva* and of his work as falling upon us from some great Himalayan height.
8. Taylor, 321
9. Taylor, 322
10. JMN VIII, 165–166
11. L III, 10
12. L III, 12
13. JMN VII, 165

## CHAPTER 10

1. A brief bibliography of Emerson's reading in scientific matters would include:
Arago, *Biographies of Distinguished Scientific Men,* 1857
Bigelow, *American Medical Botany,* 1820
Brewster, *Memoirs of Newton,* 1855
Brightwell, *Life of Linnaeus,* 1858
Brown, *Lectures on Atomic Theory,* 1858
Chambers, *Vestiges of the Natural History of Creation,* 1845
Dalton, *A Treatise on Human Physiology,* 1859
Humboldt, *Cosmos,* 1847
James, Henry, Sr., *Substance and Shadow,* 1863
Lardner, *Cabinet Cyclopaedia*
Linnaeus, *Lachesis Lapponica,* 1839
Martins, *Metamorphose des Plantes*
Owen, *Palaeontology,* 1860
Prichard, *Natural History of Man*
Stewart, *Elements of the Philosophy of the Human Mind*

2. L. III 19–20
3. L. III, 20
4. L. III, 28
5. L. III, 29, 30
6. L III, 89
7. L. III, 90–91
8. L. III, 146
9. L. III, 149

## CHAPTER 11

1. JMN XI, 412
2. JMN XIV, 375
3. JMN XI, 344
4. *Miscellanies,* "Theodore Parker," Wm. H. Wise, NY, p. 1207
5. JMN VII, 155

## CHAPTER 12

1. Anne Lamott, *Bird by Bird,* Pantheon, 1994, p. 99
2. Eric Voegelin, *Anamnesis* (University of Missouri Press, Columbia and London, translated and edited by Gerhart Niemeyer, 1978), p. 103
3. Ibid, p. 196
4. Giovanna Borradori, *The American Philosopher,* University of Chicago Press, 1994, p. 130
5. JMN IV, 7

## EPILOGUE

1. The reference here is to the oracle which said: "Sophocles is wise, Euripides wiser, but wisest of all is Socrates." Socrates, of course, claimed that he knew nothing. For Emerson, this connection between wisdom and modesty was essential.
2. *Select Works of Plotinus,* 344
3. JMN XV, 8
4. Cameron, K.W., *Ralph Waldo Emerson's Reading,* Haskell House, New York, 1973, 18
5. JMN III, 213n
6. JMN III, 236n

# WORKS CITED

Bloom, Harold, *Omens of the Millennium,* New York: Riverhead, 1996.

————*The American Religion,* New York: Touchstone, 1992.

Cavell, Stanley, *Must We Mean What We Say?,* Cambridge: Cambridge University Press, 1976.

————*Conditions Handsome and Unhandsome,* Chicago: University of Chicago Press, 1990.

Cameron, K.W., *Ralph Waldo Emerson's Reading,* New York: Haskell House, 1973.

Channing, William E., *The Works of William E. Channing,* Boston: Monroe & Co., 1841.

Geldard, Richard, *The Esoteric Emerson,* Hudson: Lindisfarne Press, 1993.

Gillman, W.H. et al., eds., *The Journals and Miscellaneous Notebooks of Ralph Waldo Emerson,* 16 volumes, Cambridge: Harvard University Press, 1960 –1982.

Godwin, Joscelyn, *The Theosophical Enlightenment,* Albany: SUNY Press, 1994.

Holmes, Oliver Wendell, *Emerson,* New York: Chelsea House, 1980. Introduction: Joel Porte.

Howe, Irving, *The American Newness,* Cambridge: Harvard University Press, 1986.

James, William, *Essays in Religion and Morality,* Cambridge: Harvard University Press, 1982.

Konvitz, Milton R., *The Recognition of Ralph Waldo Emerson,* Ann Arbor: University of Michigan Press, 1972.

Lamott, Anne, *Bird By Bird,* New York: Pantheon, 1994.

Orth, Ralph H. et al, eds., *The Topical Notebooks of Ralph Waldo Emerson,* Columbia: University of Missouri Press, 1990.

Paramananda, Swami, *Emerson and Vedanta,* Vedanta Center, 1918.

Porte, Joel, *Representative Men,* New York: Oxford University Press, 1979.

Richardson, Robert D., Jr., *Emerson: The Mind on Fire,* Berkeley: University of California Press, 1995.

Rusk, Ralph, ed., *The Letters of Ralph Waldo Emerson,* volumes 1–6, New York: Columbia University Press, 1939.

Slater, Joseph et al., eds., *The Collected Works of Ralph Waldo Emerson.* 5 volumes, Cambridge: Harvard University Press, 1971.

Taylor, Thomas, trans., *Select Works of Plotinus,* London: 1817.

Voegelin, Eric, *Anamnesis,* Columbia: University of Missouri Press, 1978.

# INDEX